To:

SABAST

WITH SINCERE BEST WISHES

Tony Steele

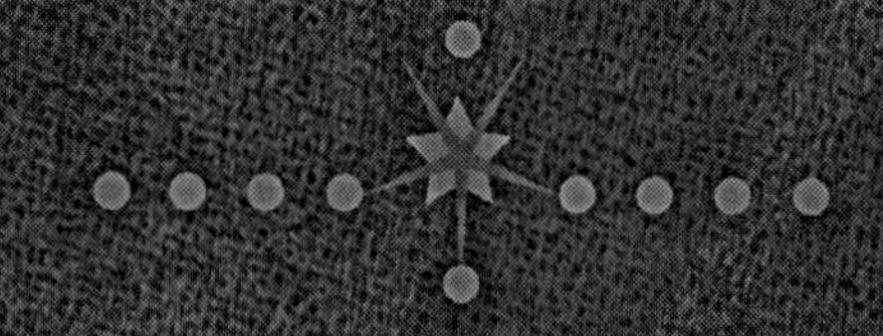

Circus Scott, Sweden 1972
TONY STEELE

You can do anything you want to do.

Things are appointed.

There is a God.

Take a chance.

Spread your wings.

Leave the nest.

Just do it.

Live fearlessly.

Be courageous.

You belong here.

- *Tony Steele*

FROM GAZOONIE TO GREATNESS

FROM GAZOONIE TO GREATNESS

A Personal Interview with

Legendary Trapeze Artist

and

World Record Holder,

Tony Steele

PAULA BLACKWELDER

REALITY CLASSICS

$20.00 WORTH EVERY PENNY

Published by Reality Classics, USA

Designer: Sherri Mann

Author: Paula Blackwelder

Blackwelder, Paula.

From gazoonie to greatness: a personal interview with legendary Trapeze artist and world record holder, tony steele / Paula Blackwelder. - 1st ed.

ISBN: ISBN 978-0-578-15129-8

Personal reality 2. Absolute possibilities 3. Motivation 4. Inspiration 5. True story 6. Happiness.

www.FromGazoonieToGreatness.com

Dedication

I dedicate this book to my family. You have allowed me countless hours on this project, to get information from Tony and do with it as he requested—to help other people.

John you encouraged me to write this book about Tony's life. You believed I needed to do this. You have been by my side, as I spliced, inserted, rearranged and deleted things. You were so patient, waiting for me to finish the last chapter. I thank you for all of your help, suggestions and of course, all of your coaching. Thank you for sharing. Thank you for teaching and thank you for your love.

Johnny you always kept yourself occupied while I wrote, and I noticed all the good choices you made while I worked on this project. You have been incredibly understanding as I took this "assignment" and ran with it, and also as I flew with it, across the country, to pitch this book. Thanks for being such a good son, while I work.

Sam you are the one who came up with the title of this book! I have enjoyed your contributions and the view-points you have given me on this. We have learned together, shared together and speak the same language—write on! I will always remember our excitement, our nervousness and our laughable encounters in Portland!

Shadiya you always believe in me, no matter what. I thank you for believing in me on this project as well. I feel your support with me as I pour myself into this project. Thank you for your acceptance, your love, and all your smiles!

Arielle your positive, happy and calming spirit has motivated me to attempt to stay that way (as much as I can) on this project. Thanks for being you and for sending sweet texts while I've worked on this. Your texts have always come at the best times while I wrote "Uncle Tony's" book.

Mom, you are the prayer warrior extraordinaire. I have felt your prayers while I have written and pitched this book, matched up pictures and interviewed characters, and even the time when the entire book was lost in cyberspace. You have taken care of so many things, just so I could complete this book. You believe in this and I feel your love and support.

I truly thank and love each of you.

Tony, I'm so glad God brought us together. It's incredible how you lived with my parents in Germany 55 years ago, you flew where I flew and who I flew with 25 years ago and now it's our turn to be together. It's our turn to fly together.

Dedication

We have prayed together, flown together, cried together, baked together, shopped together and have taken the wrong roads together. You listen to me when I scold you. You listen to me when I cry. You have helped me pull out of so many things. You have helped me understand. Thank you for being there for me. Thank you for simplifying. Thanks for your smile.

Enough with the mushies, we've got work to do!

With supernatural love,

Paula

Oh, and God, I know you arranged my accident so I would sit still long enough to write Tony's book. I hope it helps people and I hope this makes you proud.

Acknowledgements

I would like to thank Sherri Mann – fellow flyer, founder of Embrace Adrenaline Flying Trapeze Club (mntrapeze.com), flying coach and graphic designer – for putting this book together. I would also like to thank Illinois State University, especially Maureen Brunsdale, Head Librarian for Special Collections and Mark Schmitt, Senior Library Specialist in Special Collections for Illinois State University's, Milner Library. Their cooperation for helping with the valuable pictures of Tony is a giant contribution to this book.

I am also grateful to the "test group" who were the first to give of their time, honesty and correction: Lisa Weathersbee, Frankie Martin, Gary Martin, Fred Putney, Betty Putney, Sam Zimmerman, and Bob Thomason, as well as Manuel Zuniga for his ideas, which I did use in this publication.

And a special recognition to Merissa Green, the final editor of this book, a.k.a. "The Book Butcher." Green is a 13 year newspaper reporter, covering stories that made the world news, such as the Abraham Shakespeare murder investigation in 2009.

"What People are Saying About Tony Steele"

Sam Keen

Author: Fire in the Belly
Learning to Fly

(Noted Author, Sam Keen began flying on the Trapeze at the age of 70.) -

"Tony Steele came to visit me one day and ended up staying for a couple of enchanted years. In his prime, Tony was the greatest flyer in the world. He did every trick Codona did, plus the 3 1/2 to the legs. But he had fallen on hard times and had all but given up flying. But once he settled into a small playhouse on my farm and began to practice every day, he soon was throwing many of his old tricks again. He was the guru and delight of a small group of flyers who played and practiced several times a week. Although he was nearly 60 years in age, he had the spirit of a child. He was always trying out new tricks, like a double birdie, to the catcher and back to the pedestal, all while telling corny jokes. From early to late, Tony was generous to all. He gave freely of his knowledge and taught anyone who desired to learn. He taught me how to find joy in discipline. It took us 93 attempts before we could catch the double with any regularity. It was a delight to have him as my teacher and friend."

Dan Thurmon, CSP, CPAE
Author: Off Balance On Purpose
Hall of Fame Speaker
Member of Speakers Roundtable
President, Motivation Works, Inc.
Atlanta, Georgia -

"It is impossible to meet Tony Steele (or read his book) without feeling uplifted and more capable than ever before! His incredible life and indelible spirit will inspire your next breakthrough and change you forever."

Maureen Brunsdale,
Special Collections Librarian
Illinois State University
Normal, Illinois -

"Tony Steele is one of the Legendary Greats. Being the first to complete the 3 1/2 somersault from the fly bar to a catcher puts him in this category. For me, it's his great capacity to teach those of us who will never reach his stratosphere and doing so with his lovable elfin spirit, that will forever keep him in the pantheon of 'Best Ever' performers. Body of Steele, heart of Gold. That one sentence sums up who Tony is to me."

Giovanni Livera
Author: Live a Thousand Years, Have the Time of Your Life -

"Tony Steele in an inspiration. His spirit for flying and

life ignites the untapped potential in all of us to reach higher."

Jean Schulz

Board President, Charles M. Schulz Museum in Santa Rosa, CA -

"I first met Tony flying on Sam Keen's rig here in California. What enchanted me about Tony was his boyish pleasure in everything he did. He and Sam would try and try again to catch Tony's dazzling tricks–and Sam felt like a pro when he was able to catch Tony. There was pure joy on that rig when Tony was there.

All of us wanted to emulate Tony's joy in flying, and he "taught" us with positive reinforcement (works with people as well as with dogs!) I still can see Tony's lithe figure in my mind and I remember what he told me about a 'take-off.'"Trapeze artists are snobs,' he said, as he brushed a finger along the bridge of his nose and up into the air. 'Take off with pride.'"

Armando Gaona

Member of the World Famous Flying Gaona's and International Circus Performer Extraordinaire

"Tony is a beautiful person and a helpful Trapeze teacher; simply one of the greatest. He would come watch us practice and give us lessons, in the beginning when we were first learning the Trapeze and putting our act together. We went to Europe and became successful. My brother, Tito was another who mastered the triple somersault. Tony would come watch us perform and was so gracious to my family. He loved to help us and he admired us. That meant a lot to us, because he is a famous person."

Al Light M.S., P.E.S.
Head Coach of Acrobatics, Cirque du Soleil - KA

"Tony Steele epitomizes grit, determination, and the courage it takes to be a true pioneer. He taught me universal truths such as 'Anything can be accomplished once you truly decide to do it.' - and - 'You, are in most cases, only limited by yourself.' He has been the most profound influence on my career, as well as an immeasurable influence of six decades of performers of every level."

Here's the Truth

"I really don't want to expose my insane life too much, but if this will help someone–that's why I did it, because this is the only purpose for this book in my mind. I don't need to be famous or notorious.

My wife Lily, of 38 years, passed away in 1996 of cancer and she was a really big part of my life, more than anyone else. Just like the Bible says; we were one. So after she passed away, I really didn't give a damn about anything, because she was such a big part of me. So I started drinking and spiraling downwards. I no longer had any goals or interest in life; absolutely none. So I got an invitation from my friend John Zimmerman in Haines City, Florida. I had been staying with friends in California, but went to visit John for 10 days, and now I've been here for almost 10 years.

I'd like to say how good John was and is to me. And the setup he has in the backyard–it's a playground for acrobatic adults. I found out that I was happy here, and being among all the aerial, Circus equipment, I found out that my grief subsided by playing and practicing on the Flying Trapeze. I discovered this was a good place for me.

Besides having the aerial rigging here to help me, I gave my car away with the purpose of stranding myself. So best of all, that combination of the remoteness of John's compound, along with being miles from the liquor store, with no vehicle, gave me the opportunity to seriously practice my craft, which I love–the Flying Trapeze, in a more devoted and playful manner. Since I'm no longer being forced to perform daily as a professional, I am able to exercise and practice my passion. It's better than stress-free, better than 'without pressure.' My lifetime labor of Trapeze has now become a happy hobby!

I'm also gaining joy and youth by giving back my knowledge to the younger people, through the Circus Schools and Circus Camps, by seeing the smiles on their faces. It's time for me to help other people on their journey. That's what we are here to do–help other people on this planet. I've had a great life. I've done everything I've wanted to do.

But I have to say, I really love John. He has helped me. He has saved my butt, so-to-speak. I joke with him all the time, that if it wasn't for him, I would be back in Reno passed out drunk behind the dumpster of the Moo Goo Gi Pan Chinese Restaurant waiting for the noodles to flow down my way. You think that's funny?–It's so close to the truth, you wouldn't believe it.

Therefore when Lily died, my thinking, that my life and the interest in it was completely gone, actually turned out to be totally incorrect. The truth is, and I'm gonna say it, the Lord Jesus has more things planned for me to do, and if people don't like it–tough!–'cause it's true."

- Tony Steele

Wenatchee Youth Circus-Washington U.S.A.
McKenzie Madland, Tony Steele, Willian "Billy" Tuthill

Forward

Many Circus books have been written over the years and these writings fall into 1 of 3 different categories. 1) Fictional, 2) Enhanced and embellished versions of real people, shows and events, 3) Factual and true accounts of the same. As an amateur, tanbark historian and connoisseur of these publications, I can say that "From Gazoonie to Greatness" is undoubtedly in the third classification. Author Paula Blackwelder has excelled in interviewing and fact checking the interesting and unbelievable life of mid-twentieth century flying Trapeze legend Tony Steele.

Although I have known Tony for 40 years, performers in their 80s and 90s today contributed information to this book. The Circus may be different today but when Tony Steele began performing at age 15, America still had many 3-ring tented extravaganzas, unbelievable characters and extremely skilled performers that lived a tough and difficult life. Circus talent had no competition from television or computers, baseball was the number one American sport and air-conditioned arenas did not exist. Many of America's greatest athletes were Circus acrobats.

If you are a Circus fan or not, you will enjoy this true story of a young man with an unusual goal and dream. He used the talents he was born with and never gave up hope to achieve his dream despite many setbacks and obstacles. He became one of the greatest in his profession and the greatest in his lifetime.

Sit down, relax, read, enjoy, and learn something to make your dreams come true, no matter what they are! --John Zimmerman

Tony Steele and John Zimmerman

Introduction

What measures would you take to go after your dream? World Record holder, Tony Steele, took extreme measures to get his dream to come true. He had to make a colossal move.

You may have a dream yet to be fulfilled. Deep down you know you'll have to make a move too, accompanied by a leap of faith, in order for it to happen for you as well.

At the age of 15, Steele grabbed the hand of faith and took a giant leap; a leap of 1,800 miles, to be exact.

Steele's dream was to become a Circus Performer. Not only was his dream realized quickly, but that dream magnificently exceeded his expectations and the expectations of anyone else. After being told he would never be a Trapeze Artist, Steele landed in the Guinness Book of World Records, only 11 years later, as the first to accomplish specific Trapeze tricks. He is a legendary Circus Artist, recognized in the famous "Ring of Fame" in Sarasota, Florida and continues to be in demand as a guest aerial instructor among Circus-art institutions, worldwide.

Steele took the first step to his dream at the age of 15. Now, at the age of 78, he is still enjoying his dream, and basking in the reality of his fantasy. No matter what step you're on in your dream coming true, "From Gazoonie to Greatness" will inspire you to go the rest of the way, and to keep moving through each step until the door to which those steps lead you, is opened.

It can be done. It has been done. Steele did it.
Trust. Believe. Fly. Soar.

Tony Steele, Ring of Fame Inductee 2010

Contents

Contents

Gazoonie (noun):

"An old, slang word from the old-time Circus - roustabout, a fly-by-night, they come and go, young, inexperienced. Tony Steele, Gunther Gebel-Williams and a lot of great 'show people' started as a working man - a Gazoonie. They were poor, but became famous. Gazoonies are not original Circus people born into the business. Those of them, who became stars, worked for it. Sometimes, the 'amateur' is better than the 'professional' because they do it out of love. The oustiders have to prove themselves."

Tomi Liebel, Circus owner,
Budapest, Hungary

Other spellings:
Gazoony
Gazooney
Gazooni

When Going For Your Dream, Is Your Best Option

Legendary Trapeze Artist and World Record holder, Tony Steele was 15 years of age when he made the decision to go after his dream. Steele's dream was to be a great aerialist in the Circus Industry. Before the advent of multiple, satellite television channels, 3-D motion pictures and electronic games consisting of international players, the Circus was one of the few resources of entertainment to bring smiles and delight to the population of the world.

Steele was inspired by the great, Norma Fox, single Trapeze superstar and Ringling Brothers Circus performer. Ringling Bros. Barnum and Bailey Circus performed in Boston every year where Steele resided.

"I was fifteen when I saw my first Circus and was just mesmerized by a beautiful, young lady who worked under the stage-name, "La Norma"; her real name is Norma Fox. I not only fell in love with her, but with the whole ambience of the Circus, and even the smell of the sawdust on the ground. I knew right away that I wanted to be in the Circus. I was certain. Most kids say, 'I want to be a fireman or a policeman or an astronaut' when they grow up, but then they may or may not go in a different direction and they also might get influenced by their parents to do other things with their lives, but this was my childhood dream and fantasy," he said.

Steele had a dream, but didn't know how to make it come true. He wanted to follow in La Norma's foot steps, and nothing else could substitute. Steele began his dream-journey with step one. He simply asked.

"I just wanted to be a Circus performer and didn't know how. I even wrote a letter to John Ringling North. I said, 'I want to be in the Circus,'" Steele said. "I asked him if there were any books about how to become a Single Trapeze artist like La Norma Fox. The Flying Trapeze was only secondary to me then. Mr. North did write back and said he was sorry he didn't know of any books, but he wished me the best of luck. That was a letter I should have kept. It had the big Ringling seal on it. You can imagine, like how kids are affected by getting an autograph by someone famous. It was the same thing to me; with the Ringling seal on there. Me, as a 15 year-old kid–I can't even tell you."

Although the Ringling letter was golden to Steele, it did not bring him any closer to his dream becoming reality. Steele began to teach himself tricks on a Single-Trapeze bar that he would hang in a tree located in a nearby park. The first trick he taught himself was the famous and thrilling ankle drop.

It was later that he learned of a community Circus in Gainesville, Texas and realized that would be a good place to start. Still only 15 yeas of age, he "ran away" from Boston, and left behind a life that would not contribute to the reaching of his goal.

"I was in an orphanage from age 10-14. My older brother Richard was there, too. He was there for three years. It cost $30 in those days to have both us boys in the orphanage; $15 each per month–room, board, education. My mother finally couldn't pay, so the priest dropped us off at the last known address," Steele said.

The timing for him to leave was right. He left Boston with basically "nothing," but only a few years would go by, and Steele would have surprisingly more than just "something."

"I had my mother's blessings. She didn't want to interfere so she gave me her blessings. She knew that is what I would have to do in order to do what I wanted to do, and become what I wanted to be. So she wrapped my lunch in a road map and sent me on my way. It was really a miracle. It was a God thing. When you think about it, that is so outrageous. You just can't do that with your kids today. You would never get away with that. I left home with a toothbrush, comb, a bar of soap, a pair of jeans and two T-shirts. I might have had $10 in my pocket. I took the Greyhound bus," Steele said.

With his Christian upbringing and being exposed to a faith in God, Steele took his spiritual strengths and beliefs with him on the road.

"I had nothing; literally nothing, but I had absolutely no concern about anything. I just knew I would be alright. I didn't even have a place to stay. I was a fifteen year-old kid, and I made it from Boston, Massachusetts to Gainesville, Texas with really, nothing. What are the odds of that? When you talk about God taking care of you!" he said with a shaking head. "When I think about it, I wouldn't have survived without God. I only had $10 in my pocket to last me for an indefinite period of time."

Steele had only read about the community Circus in Gainesville, Texas, but had never visited.

He said, "Like some towns have a community theater, Gainesville had a community Circus, so I went there. You talk about blind faith, baby!"

Steele would stay in the Circus barn with just a sleeping bag.

"I would get kicked out of the barn, but then I would go back. The Gil Gray show came to winter there and I told Gil Gray, the owner, that I had a Single Trapeze act and I wanted to be in his show, and he said, 'Go over there and see Shorty. He'll tell you what to do.' So I went over there to see Shorty, and he gave me a paint brush and a bucket of paint and said, 'Go over there and start on that wagon, and when you get finished there with that, I'll have something else for you to do.' So they hired me as a roustabout, but at least they had a cook-house and I could eat now. I might have made $5 a week. With my first week's pay, I can remember what I did with my first $5. I went across the street to Curtis Diner and got a piece of cherry pie with ice cream. I remember it like it was yesterday. I can still taste it. I took my whole week's salary for that."

Tony Steele Age

Top picture: Back Balance
om picture: One Hock Catch

Chapter 1

Questions for Personal Reflection

Based on Chapter 1, you now know, or have been reminded, that age is not a factor in pursuing your goal.

Steele didn't know how to get to his goal at first, but found someone, a leader in the industry he wished to belong to, and wrote a letter to that individual.

Who is in your network with whom you can communicate right now, to get you closer to your goal?

Communicate with them right now, with a sense of urgency for yourself.

Steele didn't let the lack of help from John Ringling North discourage him, instead, he took steps he thought would get him closer to reaching his goals. He taught himself tricks on the Trapeze.

Besides finishing this book, what is one thing you can do to "teach yourself" to get closer to your goal?

At the age of 15, Steele did something jaw-dropping to reach the goal he set for himself.

List some creative and outrageous things you can do right now, to move forward in realizing your goal.

Steele had to relocate to have his goal fulfilled. Make the determination now on whether or not relocation is necessary for your goal to be met.

Steele took odd jobs, made sacrifices and lived uncomfortably on the way to reaching his goal. These are also things you may have to endure as well.

When You Least Expect It

As Steele was starting out his dream with nothing, washing his jeans and shirt on a rock, with only a bar of soap was common for him. While laundering his clothes in this fashion one day, the uncommon happened.

"Gil Gray decided to put me in the flying act as a clown. He said I was going in and comedy was good," Steele said.

But that didn't fair well with the members of the troupe in this Trapeze act, also known as the flying act.

Steele said, "They despised me, hated me and wanted to kill me. They didn't want anyone to change or interfere with their fancy flying act. They were a classic flying act, called the "Flying Malkos" and comedy wasn't their thing."

According to Steele, the members of the troupe were Mike Kocuik, June Malcom and Jeep Milan; one of the most outrageous characters Steele remembers from his early Circus days.

"Jeep was the most 'sensational' flyer whoever lived.

His form was terrible. He was terrifying to watch! The people would scream!," Steele said. "If you can image throwing a lobster up in the air by one claw, that's what Jeep looked like when he flew."

Describing the aerial skills of Milan, Steele recalls Milan doing a trick called the "forward-over."

"He did a forward over and he would lift so late and drop three feet and just barely catch it by the finger tips," Steele said. "The full twist was the best. He never got a full twist. He got a half in. He would catch the trick with one hand behind him and the catcher would catch up with the other hand at about center. I never saw anybody fly like him. Oh, what a character he was; geesh! He would do the fliffus (a double somersault with a half twist to the stick) with a lay-out back," Steele said. "It was the ugliest, most awkward, death-defying thing I have ever seen. Then Jeep would stay out there in the ring, styling through the next two acts. He really thought he was something. He was just a real diva."

Now Steele was about to be a part of this side of the show. From painting ring curbs and cleaning up after animals, to working with show-offs and egotistical performers, Steele was entering the world for which he had been dreaming.

Steele said, "Jeep was little, I think less than five feet. He was an arrogant and stuffy type of person. He used to style and stay out there in the ring through the next act and everyone else would leave and he would just stay there. He would give flying advice to other people too. People would say, 'How can I improve my trick, Jeep?' and he would say, 'If you get a chance, hurry up.'" He was so stiff 24 hours per day, he would just give answers that way. I don't even know what he meant. That's just like, if someone asked Bob Christians, 'How can I improve this trick?' He would say, 'A little more of everything.'"

Christians was a highly respected gymnast who attended Florida State University, and who took Steele's place in the Malkos Flying Act, when he was drafted into the United States Army in 1959.

"What I learned from Jeep was, do the opposite of everything he did. That sounds mean, but it's true," Steele said.

Being only at the young age of 15, Steele was fascinated and spellbound by this man he was about to join on the pedestal board and perform with in front of the crowds.

He said, "Jeep was only yay-big, but he was a womanizer and he was a terrible alcoholic. He thought he was a great flyer, but he had no acrobatic skills or abilities. He just did the tricks with sheer guts and defiance. But the goose got to him, finally. All of a sudden he started figuring out how bad he was. He lost his nerve. The alcohol made him scared. He just couldn't take it any more. He just got horrified. If they had videos back then, and he saw himself, he would have quit a lot earlier. Oh, God bless him. I feel bad talking about him. Is it a sin to talk about someone after they've gone? There was no such thing as form back then, and he sure didn't have any."

When Milan quit, Steele said that's when he began learning. Before that time, Steele said he was held back.

"I was not allowed to do anything. Nobody would dare step on Jeep's toes because he was the diva," Steele said. Mike Malko taught me how to fly. Also in the show was Billy Woods and Slick Valentine as roustabouts, and we all wanted to fly. THIS IS THE BEST PART OF MY ENTIRE LIFE AND I LIKE IT BECAUSE IT'S TRUE AND IT'S FUNNY. What we did was, all the stage-hands were friends of ours, and they would set the net up, and we would go up and practice in secret in between shows when the performers were off the lot. We had an Indian friend who used to watch the door and he would give a whistle in case the boss was coming. They would drop the net, roll it up and we would lay on top of the net and start playing cards on it. It got to be so amusing after a while. It got to be a cat and mouse game. The performers would go inside the buildings to shower and use the bathroom and they would see us flying and they would go back and tell Mike Malko that we were practicing flying and Mike never believed them because when he would come in the building he would never catch us. We would always be on the ground playing cards or something. We got faster and faster and more giggly, until one day, he came in and the same thing happened, and there we were playing cards and he turned around to walk out, then turned back around again, and he looked up and saw the Trapeze bar swinging all by itself. We had made a mistake. We were caught and that was while Jeep was still in the act," Steele said.

"But all that changed when Jeep Milan left. All of a sudden, everybody could practice because Mr. Gray needed more flyers and more people. The proof is, now he had so many available people, that the next year, he made a double-wide flying Trapeze act with Billy Woods, Raymond "Slick" Valentine, myself and anybody else who could fly. Jeep was a thing of the past and there will never be another like him."

Russell Nafus, June Malko, Jeep Milan, Mike Malko

Chapter 2

Questions for Personal Reflection

As you go for your dream, remember—your luck can change in an instant; what a difference one day can make. Expect goodness to happen. Keep in mind, it is on its way to you.

List one positive phrase, or even an encouraging Bible verse that you can have available to you at all times to remind yourself of this.

The same thing that happened to Tony Steele, can happen to you. Not everybody is going to like you, but you may still have to work together.

Make a plan for how you will react and behave if you find yourself in the company of the jealous or prudish, especially having to work with them on a daily basis.

Ever been held back from progressing forward like Tony was? It may happen again.

What is your plan if someone in a more powerful position than you, exercises their capacity to hold you back?

The People Who Will Enter Your Life!

See, they had characters in those days. Nobody is a character any more, ya know? Everybody is normal," Steele said. "Slick had a broken neck. He fell bad in the net. He would walk around with his head tilted all the time and he is the one we used to use, to level our crane bars. Can you imagine that? His head was titled all the time, and he is telling us if our rigging is straight! He had a broken leg too. He accomplished that coming off the net on a web to swing down, and hit the ring curb, but we used to tell people he broke it jumping out of a two story window of the house of a woman he had been with, the time her husband came home."

Slick Valentine said he caught Steele many, many times, and that he and Steele did a flying act, when his son, Raymond Valentine Jr. dislocated his shoulder.

"When Tony came in, we called it the 'Over the Hill Gang' because we were all in our forties. It was just amazing," Valentine said.

Steele remembers Slick Valentine fondly, and always with a belly full of laughs. Steele said he was most impressed with his continuance; never letting anything stop him or slow him down. Slick Valentine simply, "just did it."

"He did a full-twist back to the fly bar, from the catch trap, and he never missed," Steele said. "Somebody bet him he couldn't do it without the net, and he said 'I'll do it without the net!' They took the net down - and he missed. That was either the Christiani Show or the Clyde Beatty Show."

Valentine was called by Ringling long after he retired to catch for the Gaonas Flying act. When he arrived at the show, the producers asked him how long it would take until the flying act would be ready.

Valentine replied, "As soon as I can get these tights on."
They were not confident in that answer, and they asked how long he would need to practice.

Valentine said, "Do they know how to fly?"

The producers told him, "Yes, they are the Gaonas."

Valentine replied, "We'll I know how to catch, so we don't need to practice."

According to Valentine, the only thing he wasn't expecting was how the Gaonas returned to the bar, either in a half turn or a pirouette.

"Generally, most of the people in Mexico and South America, they turn to the right when they do their pirouettes and half turns. The North Americans go to the left, so that was the only thing different," Valentine said.

As Steele and Valentine reminisced, Steele recalled the time they were in the middle of a practice and he shouted to Valentine from the board, "Hey Slick, double-forward over?"; which is a trick most catchers call a nightmare since they can be kicked in the face by the flyer.

As Valentine swung nonchalantly in the catch trap, he replied back to Steele, "Never mind the mule, just load the wagon."

Steele laughs about that every time he tells that story.

Another "Slick Valentine Saga" that Steele recalls being incredibly outrageous is the time Valentine was asked to catch for the Rocksmith flyers.

Valentine said, "It was horrible! I had already been retired for 2 1/2 years, and to go up and catch without practicing; wow - I was sore. I arrived to the show during intermission. They threw a pair of tights at me. I got them on and we were up next. I was putting on my wrist bands, walking out to the ring, and as I was tying them bands in a knot with my teeth, I looked up and saw this web hanging down and I said to myself, 'Now how the hell am I going to get the hell up there?' I used to have a ladder going up to my catch trap, not a damn rope! When I finally got up there, I said, 'Well, that's about all I've got."

Valentine elaborated on his size, being robust and hefty, thus having his catch trap to suit the dimensions of his body."

"Once I got to the catch trap, I realized it was about half the size of mine. I couldn't even get in it. Once I got my legs in it, I didn't have any place to put my hands! My butt wasn't even touching the bar, and I had to put one hand on top of the other to even make a lock," he said. "Then, I turned around to see what kind of trick they were going to throw me, and they were making some kind of hand gesture and I didn't know what the hell all those hand signs meant."

Valentine said that all the tricks done by David Smith Rocksmith were caught by the legs. "His left knee would hit me in one temple and the right knee would hit me in the right temple," he said.

Valentine brought so many gutt-laughs into Steele's life; so much camaraderie, that Steele possesses delightful memories of his time "working." Valentine was his co-worker, and a member of the team, who became an unforgettable "character" in Steele's life and brought cheer and fulfillment to his daily walk on this earth. The amusement that Steele experienced with this one character brought, as Steele said, blissful, glorious moments, from teaching Valentine tricks with spoons when they were only teenagers in the Circus, to practicing never-before-attempted tricks on the Flying Trapeze.

"The cheer and charm were wonderful," Steele revealed. "Just glee; pure glee."

Valentine's opinion of Steele's life journey is clear and simple.

"Tony was in the right places at the right times," he said.

Billy Woods, Rosa Valentine, Slick Valentine

Chapter 3

Questions for Personal Reflection

Do you have any "characters" in your life like Slick Valentine? If so, keep them around. They'll keep you laughing, they'll challenge you and they'll remind you that things aren't always as bad as they may seem. If you don't have at least one "real character" in your life, get one. Humor, and over coming obstacles, like Valentine did, will keep you at your best. Do you have any characters in mind? Remember, if you want a friend, you must first, be a friend. So get a funny friend to bring you alleviation, celebration and elation.

Most professionals, who are considered to be successful, have a solid relationship with mentors and advisors in their circle. Inviting someone into your personal world, who has the gift of ebb and the ability to calmly coast, no matter what circumstances are, can be a gigantic asset to you.

Name at least one "character" in your life that you can become better acquainted with or name someone whom you think could connect you with a "real character."

Next time you are faced with a challenge like a broken neck or someone asks you to fill in for them, and you walk into that duty, blind and cold, think first of how outrageous your predicament is, and follow through with tenacity. Think now how you will respond and behave, the next time you are faced with a challenge. As long as you're alive, you will be faced with challenges; you can expect them. Make your plan and make it now.

In Spite of it All, He Made it Anyway

"This is part of my life that is very important. My father's father, threw my father off the roof of a four-story window when he was an infant. Then, he jumped. He died, but my father landed in a snow bank on a lower floor and that is what saved him. He lived–obviously, because my brother, Richard 'Dick' Steele and I, are here.

What is so interesting is that it happened right across the street from a Catholic Church (Cathedral of the Holy Cross) and they were just letting out the Mass, and the parishioners saw everything. It happened in Douchester, outside of Boston. My brother and I found out about it because my brother did some research on our father and got some newspaper clippings," Steele said.

What brought on this intrigue was a visit to the BYMCU; the Boston Young Men's Christian Union.

"I was there every day, even on Sundays, when I was 12 to 14 years old. I went there to workout on everything–trampoline, high-bar, rings; I had my single Trapeze there too. There was nothing at home to do, and getting there on the metro was half the fun. I would get that place up front by the driver, and the wind would come in. It was great, and only cost 15 cents one way. When I would be there, I would fence with Author Fox. He was the physical director, and a fencer. He would stand against the wall, and people would challenge him, but they just couldn't touch him. It was amazing!

Author said to me one day, 'You remind me of a gymnast we had here. They had an act in Vaudeville called Steele and Reede. They had a ring act and he used to do a half somersault to the feet. There's a photograph in the massage parlor. Come with me, I'll show you.'

I went upstairs and saw this picture of me. That was me! I just couldn't believe it. I said, 'Hey! That's me.' So I went home and asked my grandmother, Jane Turner, 'Who was Ernest Steele in the act, 'Steele and Reed?' She said, 'We don't talk about it.' It was actually her husband; my grandfather. He threw my father off the roof, and then he jumped to his death. A tragedy happened. So my brother got curious and did some research and found out about it. He found a Boston Globe that had the story in it.

Apparently, he and his wife, our grandparents, got into a fight and he jumped, head first to his death. He died instantly. It was January 31, 1915.

It wasn't my father's time. If it had been his time,

then that would mean my brother and I would not have existed. That is interesting to me, because people are always wondering about life and what they are doing here, then when certain events like this happen, you think, 'Well, I guess I am supposed to be here after all.'"

STEELE CHILD MAY LIVE.

Hurled From Roof by Father, Who Plunged to Death-Mrs Steele Is Expected to Recover.

David Steele, the 30-months-old son of Earnest W. Steele, who while temporarily insane hurled the chld from the roof of a house on Union Park st. is resting comfortably at the City Hospitol. Steelwas killed by plunging from the roof. Mrs. Steel, who was struck over the head with an iron blackjack by her husband, is expected to recover.

The child received injuries, which at first were thought to be fatal, but now some hopes are held out for his recovery.

STEELE CHILD MAY LIVE.
Boston Daily Globe (1872-1922) Feb 2, 1915;

Pg. 2

HURLS BABY OFF ROOF AND JUMPS
Boston Daily Globe (1872-1922) Feb 1, 1915;
pg. 1

HURLS BABY OFF ROOF AND JUMPS

Steele Instanlty Killed and Boy Is in Critical Condition.

SCENE OF TRAGEDY AT WASHINGTON AND UNION-PK STS.
Atrov points to where Steele stood when he threw the baby, and later plunged headlong to the sidewalk. Inserts - Portraits of Ernest W. Steel and Mrs Jennie Steele.

Man Runs Amuck in South End Flat --Wife Severly Cut on the Head.

Temporarily insane, Earnest William Steele, formaerly a trapeze performer, ran amuck yesterday morning, severely cut his wife's head with an improvised blackjack, threw his youngest child from the roof to the street, 35 feet below, and finally, when about to be arrested, himself plunged from the same roof into Union Park st, in full view of hundreds of horrified persons.

Steele, who was 37 years old and loived with his mother at 4 Mt Pleasant st, Roxbury, died instantly. The child, David, 20 months old, and the wife, Mrs. Jenny Steele, 28 years old, are patients at the Boston City Hospital. The boy is on the dangerous list with a broken upper jaw and concussion of the brain, and the woman has three deep cuts in the scalp.

The trouble started in suite 8, 1366 Washington st. the fourth-floor apartment, where Mrs. Steele lived with her mother. Mrs Annie Truner; her three grown brothers, Edward, William and Richard, and her two children, Richard, 3 years old, and the baby, David.

Continued on the sesond page.

HURLS BABY OFF ROOF AND JUMPS

Continued From the First Page.

Steele and his wife had not lived together for 17 months, but it was his custom to call at the house every Sunday morning to get the older child, Richard, whom he was accustomed to take to his home in Roxbury to spend the day with himself and his mother.

Strikes Wife Over Head.

When Steele arrival at the Turner household yesterday morning he seemed in an ugly mood. He objected to the way his wife cared for the younger child, David, and before many minutes the husband and wife were quarreling.

It is said Steele made a number of insulting remarks to his wife and finally drew from his pocket a heavy window cord, upon which had been threaded many iron nuts, and struck her on the head three times with this. With blood flowing from the wounds on her head, Mrs Steele sank to the floor, screaming.

Edward and William, her two brothers, rushed to her aid, and overpowering Steele after a struggle took the black jack from him. A second later, however, he wrenched himself free from their hands and grabbing up the baby, David, stepped out of a window on the Union-pk side of the house.

This window looks out on the roof of an L, three stories high. Steele ran to the edge of this and threw the baby to the street.

This was shortly after 9 o'clock and worshipers were entering and leaving the Cathedral of the Holy Cross, directly across the street. They were horror stricken to see the white bundle come flying down through the air and land in Union-pk st. Gazing up they caught sight of Steele retreating from the edge of the roof.

Those nearest rushed to the spot and picked up the blood-covered child.

Steele Forgotten.

Meanwhile Steele's mad act had been seen from inside the flat of the Turners, and Edward and William Turner came downstairs and carried the infant upstairs to the wounded and hysterical mother.

The youngest of Mrs Steele's three brothers, Richard, had gone to get a policeman, and soon came up the stairs with Sergt John Hughes of the East Dedham-st Police Station.

Hughes asked where Steele was, but none of the family seemed to know.

The last any of the Turners had seen of Steele was when he dashed into the room through the window, brandishing a long knife, and shouting: "I've got rid of one of them, and now I'll get the rest!" But he had made no effort to harm Richard or his wife's relatives, and in the excitement over the injuries of Mrs Steele and the baby, he had been forgotten.

Looking out of the window over the roof of the L Sergt Hughes saw Steele standing on the edge. Steele had a knife in his hand.

"Come here," said the sergeant.

Steele replied that the officer should come and get him.

"I don't want to hurt you," said the sergeant, "I only want to talk things over."

As he spoke the policeman got through the window to the roof and began to walk toward Steele.

Steele Jumps Head First.

Suddenly Steele dropped the knife, put his arms at his side and dove headforemost from the roof.

The whole affair had taken place inside of three or four minutes, and the same crowd which had seen the baby hurled from the roof witnessed the suicide of the father.

Patrolman Patrick Flaherty, in the street below, saw Steele dive. He was the first one to reach the limp form Steele struck the sidewalk on his head, and death was instantaneous. His head was crushed almost beyond recognition.

The ambulance of the East Dedham-st Police Station was summoned and Mrs Steele and her son were carried to the City Hospital.

At the hospital it was found that the 35-foot fall had fractured the upper jaw of the baby, which suffered from concussion of the brain as well. The assault up Mrs Steele had been productive of three nasty scalp wounds. The mother is not in a serious condition, however.

After being viewed by Medical Examiner Leary the body of Steele was taken to the City Hospital Morgue.

Misunderstandings, domestic troubles and jealousy led up to these events, according to members of the Turner family. Steele was not a drinking man, yet at times, they claim, he would have strange fits of ugliness, not unlike the mood in which he came to the house yesterday morning. The married life of the couple was happy for neither.

Out of Work of Late.

Steele at one time traveled with Ringling Brothers circus as a trapeze performer. He and partner had a disagreement, however, and he returned to Boston. Because of their domestic unhappiness, Steele and his wife separated, he going to live with his mother, in Roxbury, and she going to live with her people in the South End.

Since living with his mother, Steele had worked at times as a painter, but of late he had been out of work, and it is thought that this may have preyed on his mind.

Steele, it is said, paid scant attention to the younger child; but his devotion to his eldest born was great.

His wife told the police that several times during their married life Steele has acted queerly.

The blackjack with which Steele struck his wife is a formidable weapon. A number of thick iron nuts had been strung on a heavy window cord, which was doubled over. The result was a heavy weapon with a series of jagged edges.

The knife Steele carried had a deerfoot handle and a six-inch blade.

Steele's mother became hysterical when she learned of the tragedy.

Chapter 4

Questions for Personal Reflection

Even though Steele made a grim discovery during his pre-teen years about a hidden, family tragedy kept secret from his brother and him, he looked at it as being interesting, instead of mortifying.

Has life-changing news ever been revealed to you that was beyond startling?

How did you handle it?

During the time in Steele's life when he was changing from a boy to a man, Steele was faced with horrifying news of his grandfather's suicide and the attempted murder of his own father.

Now that you have learned about this occurrence in Steele's life and how he handled it, how might you handle alarming news if it ever finds its way to you?

Would you now have handled terrifying news differently that perhaps you mishandled in your past?

The "N" Word

Before Steele's solo journey to Gainesville, Texas, he performed as a young boy with the free Circus acts who performed in Paragon Park, located on Nantasket Beach in Hull, Massachusetts.

"My mother gave Harry Lamar permission to take me as a clown for the show. I remember as a clown, I would come out about an hour before the show started, and I would walk around like an idiot; just acting silly. Everyone watched me walk around like a fool for an hour, so it was no surprise when I came out during the flying act, clowning and cutting up," Steele said.

The flying act on this show, which traveled the northeast region of the United States, was "The Flying Lamars."

"I climbed up the ladder and they were telling me to get down, but it was all part of the act. I was clowning," Steele said.

But behind all the laughs and joking, there was something going on, that was not real funny.

"Harry Lamar told me I would never be a flyer. He had to push me into a straight trick (a non-revolving trick) just to get me to the catcher. My swing was so bad, he told me, 'Just forget it. You will never be a flyer.'" Steele said. "He constantly told me how bad I was. I was just a clown when I joined Harry LaMar and only spent one season, but it was always negative."

Although Steele went through a discouraging experience, he still held on to his dream of becoming an aerialist, and as a result of holding on to that dream, Steele ventured off to Gainesville, Texas. Once he proved himself on the Gil Gray show and "climbed the Trapeze ladder," owner of the Circus, Gil Gray, put him in the Flying Malkos flying Trapeze act, although against their will. Gray also had Steele perform in the act as a clown, but unlike his experience with the Flying Lamars, he finally had the opportunity to train on the Trapeze. He worked with the Malkos for 10 years, and the results of a decade of flying, began to surface.

"While showing in Lexington, Illinois, in 1955 in a city fair, Harry Lamar came to the show. This was 10 years later, and I was doing the triple and all those other big tricks with the Flying Malcos. He saw me and came up to me and apologized for what he had said 10 years before; that I would never be a flyer. That was a good day for me," Steele said. "He told me, 'I was wrong.' That meant more than anything to me; to have the person who told me I would never be anything at all, to say I was good."

After that day of ecstatic jubilation, Steele was on his way to the top. With confidence as his quiet companion, he began to train harder and improve even more. In 1962, just a decade after he was told he would never be a flyer, Steele would be the first Trapeze artist in history to perform the 3 1/2 somersault to a legs catch, which ultimately landed him in the Guinness Book of World Records; far from Lamar's prediction.

Never tell anyone, "never"–including yourself.

Steele says, "You can rise above anything if you put in the work and the belief."

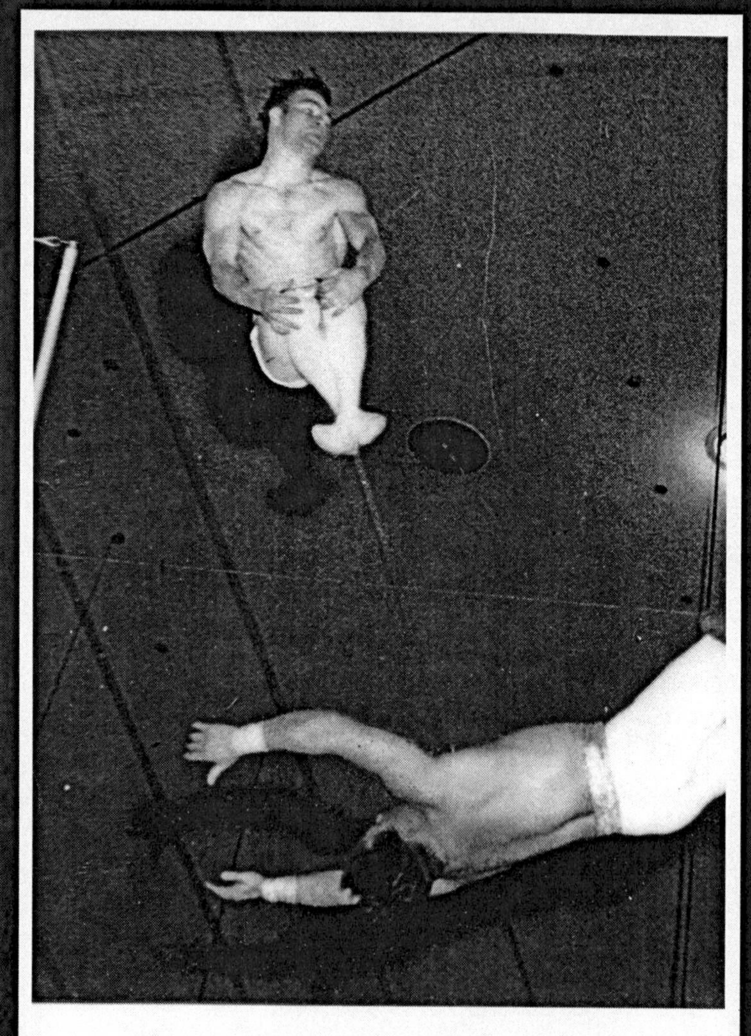

Tony Steele and Mike Malko

Trick: Double Somersault With a Full Twist – Half In, Half Out

Chapter 5

Questions for Personal Reflection

Has anyone ever given up on you? Has anyone ever told you to forget about achieving your dream?

Use the same tenacity as Steele did to ignore the nay sayers. Go for your dream. Train for what you want. Keep going. The only time you should use the "N" word, is when you say, "NEVER STOP!"

What's your plan?

You plan your parties, you plan your vacations, you plan your retirement. Now, plan your dream.

For a Reason

Tony's parents divorced when he was young. He never saw his dad, past the age of 10.

"He would visit on Sundays. We lived with Aunt Francis," he said.

His grandmother, Jane, the wife of Ernest Steele lived there too, along with his brother, Richard, who would occasionally visit their father in a bar in downtown Boston.

Steele said the absence of his father did not affect his life in either direction, negative or positive. Steele said the fact that his father was not an acting parent, had nothing at all to do with his drive and determination to become a recognizable, world-renowned flyer. Steele says the only thing that really inspired him to become a great flyer was when Harry LaMar told him to keep his day-job, because he would never become even a good flyer.

Steele always had a daring spirit, according to his younger brother Richard. These brothers resided and were schooled at the House of the Angel Guardian in West New Berry, Massachusetts. Richard remembers the outrageous shenanigans always played out by his older brother Tony.

"Tony climbed up the water pipe at the school and hung out there all night just to scare the heck out of everybody the next morning. We found an old piece of a pipe on a fence and stretched it out between two trees and he would walk it. We made the platform in such a way that we cut a hole in it, and stapled a carpet to it, that way if anyone else tried to climb the tree and walk out on the wire, they would fall through the carpet to their death before they even got to the wire. It never happened though," Richard Steele said.

At the age of 78, Steele looks back and reviews how everything in his life played out and can now be seen as dots, all being connected somehow.

Steele said, "My father landed in the snow and survived, because things happen for a reason. If my father had died, my brother and I wouldn't be here. A lot of times, I meditate, because things that have happened to me, don't happen to a lot of people. I think, 'What is my purpose?' I even pray, 'God direct me and help me to reach people.' "

History of the House of the Angel Guardian

The House of the Angel Guardian was founded in Boston, Massachusetts by Father George Foxcroft Haskins. Father Haskins was born to a wealthy Boston family and educated at Boston Latin and Harvard University.

He was ordained as an Episcopalian priest in 1830, but one decade later, would convert to Catholicism. He has been described as a friend to the poor and protector of innocence and youth. Father Haskins believed it was important to instill the Catholic faith in children and as a result, he established the House of the Angel Guardian Orphanage in 1851. It was a charitable, boarding institution for boys ages 9-16. The institution served orphans, half-orphans and those too poor to attend regular schools.

Father Haskins believed the route to a better life was through access to education. He used the same concepts of discipline and regulation found in monasteries and seminaries; prayer, chorus and music. By 1917, more than 15,000 boys were graduated.

In 1974, the school became the John C. Page School, serving West Newbury, Mass. children in elementary education, and continues to this day.

Chapter 6

Questions for Personal Reflection

Things happen in everyone's life that can be interpreted as bizarre, unexpected, unfortunate or even unfair, but as Steele looks at it–everything happens for a reason.

His father being thrown from a window as an infant, negative treatment, name calling and hopeless conditions were all part of Steele's life–at a young age, but Steele says, "Everything happens for a reason."

After reading this chapter, can you think of something that has happened in your life that you could look at now as, "happening for a reason" instead of perhaps as a "bad" thing?

A Change of Heart

While Steele was performing with the Flying Malkos the act consisted of Steele, Mike Kocuik, June Malcom and Jeep Milan. They all worked together three times at the largest Circus in Mexico–Circo Atayde. The third time there was certainly a charm for Steele.

When we got there the third time, there was a French troupe in the show called the "Therons." There was a gorgeous girl named, Lily, who had come from France to Mexico with the Ballet; not as a principle, but as a ballet dancer, with Ballet Russe.

They call Mexico the "Tomb of the Artists" because the corruption gets in and messes up the show and the shows fold. Ballet Russe folded, and Lily was with them," he said.

"She was a beauty. They loved her fair skin and her French accent. She was doing television commercials and such, and she went to the Circus and saw the Therons and went back stage and spoke with them. She was longing to speak to someone in her native tongue. They asked her to be in their act, so she joined them. Once she got settled in Mexico, she sent for her sister who was still in France. They lived in an artists' commune. It was called the Octogono. They displayed their paintings and art work there.

While Lily was on Atayde, they wouldn't let her sunbathe. Mr. Atayde saw her out sunbathing one time and said, 'No! No! No! We have plenty of brown people here. You don't sun bathe! Part of your beauty is your white, fair skin. We have enough tan people down here.'"

Steele and Lily became close friends and grew rather fond of each other. After that season on Atayde, both the Therons and the Malcos returned to the states. Both acts booked with the Polack Bros. Circus. Lily and Tony continued their friendship, and at the end of that season, the couple returned to Mexico and got married there.

"We got married by a famous preacher in Mexico City who married famous movie stars and Circus people. I went to Mexico with Lily because she had a place and I didn't. I never had a permanent place. I had so much stuff that I traveled with. It was so beautiful in Mexico back then, and I got along so good with the artists, I decided not to go back to the states. I decided I would just stay in Mexico," he said.

Steele was 23 years of age when he and Lily wed. He was also one of only two known flyers in the world who was performing the triple somersault. Lalo Palacios was the other known flyer in 1958 completing the triple.

"I got a lot of pleading from Mike Malco. George Hamid of the Hamid Morton Circus was going to sue me and all that stuff. They were advertising the triple for the shows and I wasn't going back. I was happy in Mexico," he said. "It amazes me how I could leave home into the unknown with nothing, and survive, and become so valuable that people are begging me to come back."

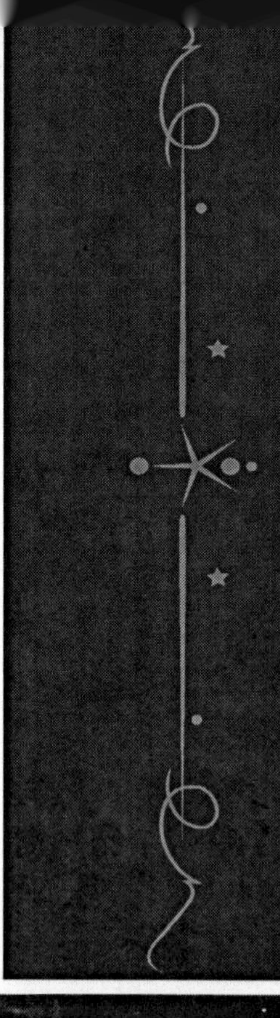

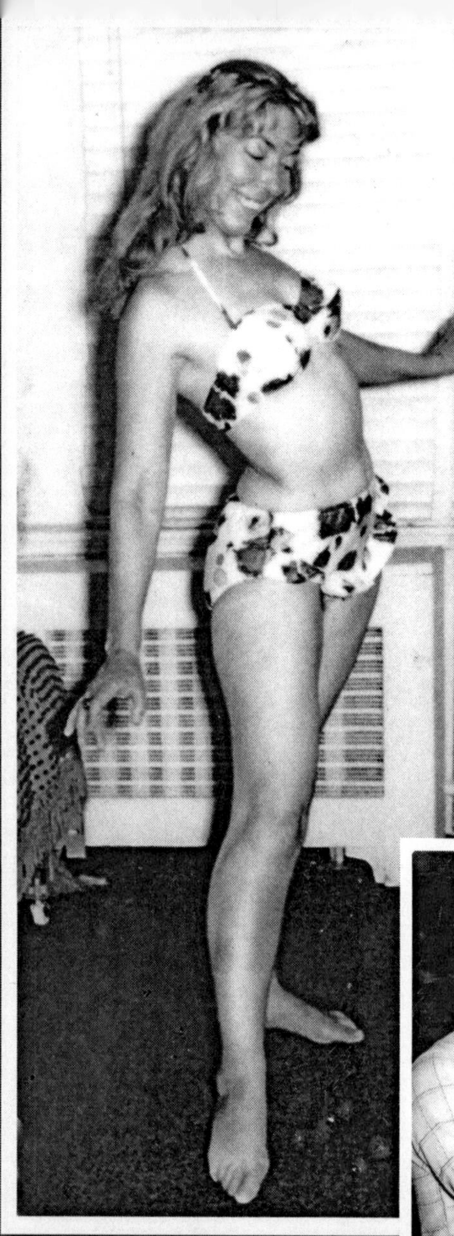

Lily Steele

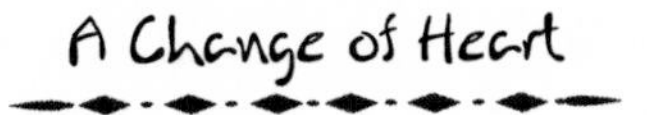

Chapter 7

Questions for Personal Reflection

Attractions come when you least expect it. Sometimes they come when you are living your dream and realizing your goal. Steele was doing this and Lily showed up.

If ever faced with that situation (and it does happen), consider how you might handle another person in your dream.

Have you ever been absolutely spell-bound by someone else's luck or success, as Steele was by La Norma Fox's in Chapter 1?

Reflect now on what that would be like to become what you wish to become, whether by serendipity or by the results of the law of cause and effect. Imagine yourself experiencing this.

Steele's childhood dream, became a hot, profitable commodity, not only for himself, but for show producers and agents. When one does not give up, this happens.

If you're not going to give up, then be prepared for your good fortune to come.

This Wasn't In The Plans

Steele finally returned to the states, but much to his surprise, he wouldn't stay there long.

"I did come back in time for the beginning of the season, because I guess I came to my senses. It occurred to me that I had to think of other things besides myself and my pleasures, but I was absolutely in love with Mexico City. Oh my God, I loved it! But when I returned, at first the management of the Hamid-Morton Circus was nice to me, then they started with the threats. That was in January 1959. That same year, I got drafted in August. I received a letter of greeting that read, 'Welcome!, You have been inducted into the United States Army,'" he said. "Mike Malco drove me to the induction center in Boston, and I never saw him again. While I was in the Army, Mike got electrocuted while working on something under his trailer at a church festival in Clifton, New Jersey.

Lily had been staying with my mother and father in Boston-Dorchester while I had to go through basic training and communication school. They then sent me to Germany, and Lily joined me. I was making $96 a month and she was making $125 just being my wife. The dependents made more than the soldiers did. I lived just off post. Certain German families would rent housing to the GIs. We were in the attic actually, the upper room, on Danziger Straße, just a few houses down from your mother and father. Isn't that funny?! (Steele speaking to the author of the book, Paula Blackwelder, during this interview.)

I was a soldier, but there was no war going on. We actually had Saturdays and Sundays off in the Army. So I made the most of this unplanned interruption in my life. We would go to the park in Friedberg. It was by an airport with gliders. There was a beautiful castle, the same one they used as the design for Disneyland. It was a little town up on the hill.

We found a tree perfect for the Trapeze; just perfect. It was another 'God thing.' The tree had a limb that was just perfect to hang the Trapeze bar, and the other tree was perfect for the safety belt. It had a perfectly level branch at about 4 ft. higher than the Trapeze branch, 12 feet away, which is the perfect distance. The branch was 12 foot out. The Trapeze and the safety belt both fit into a large suit case and it just barely fit on our bicycle. We had people hold the safety lines. We would do layouts, doubles and even triples. Every Saturday and Sunday we would do that to keep up our skills.

Every night I would go home, off post, and think that the Army was miserable because it wasn't the Circus, but when I think about it now, I was in the Army with

Elvis Presley, and I even tagged him out at first base during a softball game. That is my claim to fame by being in the US Army. I made the most of it and made some memories, too."

Thursday, April 6, 1961 THE STARS AND STRIPES

Acrobatic Homework

Pfc David Steele and wife Lilly work out on chinning bar in their one-room flat. —S&S Photo

PFC Steele Taking Part In Exercise

GRAFENWOHR, GERMANY (AHTNC) — Army PFC David A. Steele, 24, son of Mrs. Alberta B. Stowe, 31 S. Monroe terrace, Dorchester, is participating with other personnel from the 3d Armored Division's 27th Artillery in a field training exercise in Grafenwohr, Germany. The artillery's phase of the training is scheduled to end April 18.

The exercise is designed to provide training under cold weather conditions during day and night maneuvers. The Grafenwohr training area is the largest training site available to NATO forces in Europe. The 3d is one of five U.S. divisions in NATO's "Pyramid of Power."

Steele is a switchboard operator in the 27th's Headquarters Battery in Friedberg. He entered the Army in August 1958 and completed basic training at Fort Benning, Ga.

Tony Steele- United States Army

Elvis Presley- United States Army

Tony and
Lily Steele

Freidberg, Germany 1959

Chapter 8

Questions for Personal Reflection

If there hasn't been anything in your life that has happened out of your control yet, it will, just as it did in Tony's case with the draft. Along that unexpected turn in the road, that he thought he had paved for himself, Steele sought for resources, like the trees, to help him keep connected to what he had much rather be doing–fulfilling his dream.

When it comes time for you to recite the Serenity Prayer, remember to get familiar with your surroundings and stay resourceful. Usually bends in the road straighten out over time and most often do not become the end of the road.

In addition, while you are temporarily detoured, find things along that way which could create a different view, and help you see your situation differently. Identify with things that are filled with humor and will be a lasting, positive memory that you will be able to smile at in the later years to come.

Whatever situation you are currently in now, list the top five things about your circumstances for which you can be thankful.

When the Curve in the Road, Curves Again

Steele served in the United States Army from August 1959 through August of 1961.

"I actually got out a few weeks early. I got special orders to go to Japan. Didn't even have to take the boat; they flew me back. Lee Stath, my catcher of the three-and-a-half with the Flying Marilees, had an engagement in Tokyo. It began the middle of August, and I wasn't supposed to get out until the end of August. All the troops were in the field and I was on rear-detachment. We were on guard-duty two hours, and off for four hours.

A jeep came and relieved me early. They said I was getting out; that I was needed somewhere else–Tokyo. A man by the name of Mr. Butz, apparently had the power to change my orders. He was the owner of the German Circus called Circus Berlin, and it was touring Japan. He had what was called the Gold Cross with the German Government. That's all I know about it. It gave him some kind of clout. They called me to the office and asked me if I would like to go on a world tour. You won't believe it, but from the time I got out, they flew me back to Ft. Dicks in New Jersey and discharged me.

Here I am right out of the Army, and went and joined Lee Stath and his wife Mary, across from Madison Square Garden, at the Belvedere. Lily was with me. Within a couple of days, we were on our way to Tokyo, via Paris and Hamburg, and over the Pole, but we never made it. We crashed in Hamburg. It was because of a wheel section that locked and tore the whole wheel off the plane, right at take-off. We were just going to lift and the wheel came off.

I know the exact sadness that I had that day, but I did not experience fear, just sadness. This fuselage just went up and crashed. I knew we were dead. No doubt about it. Then we looked at ourselves and said, 'We are alive!' Let's get the hell off this plane! Lily was seated behind me. She removed her seat belt and flew on top of me.

The planes have names. The name of this plane was called the Pali' de Versaille' from AirFrance. Years later, the pilot wrote about it. We jumped off the plane into mud. There were no chutes in those days. We ran across the field, and the plane burst into flames. Of course I saw God in it. We could have been killed! This great, big, enormous thing crashed! I was only 25 years old. Lee and Mary may have been 10 years older. I realize now, looking back on that day, that I had a lot more things to do. Everything I have done in my life since that plane crash, I realize I have touched a lot of people. I don't think there was a reason for the crash. I've come to the conclusion that things just happen. So instead of dying at the age of

25, I have lived past the age of 75. That is more than 50 years. I have entertained people all over the world, and trained people. Some folks are preachers, but I think our God-thing was to entertain people; which we did."

La même de plus prés, remarquez le déchirement de la tôle eu sectionnement

Same view a little nearer, note the destruction of sheet metal collapse of the sl[...] into sec[...]

Vue opposée, le personnels de secours contrôle l'extinction des instruments électriques à bord. Notez la porte avant droite ainsi que l'issue de secours sur l'aile par lesquelles les membres de l'équipage ont fait évacuer les passagers

Sur l'ensemble des personne à bord seuls 8 seront blessées, dont un gravement, il s'agit du Commandant Tuduri lui même, victime d'une fracture de la colonne vertébrale mais rassurez vous, il a repris le manche et fini sa carrière chez Air France, vous voulez faire se connaissance, cliquez dessous.

If you wish to contact him, Click here

Et ce dernier, s'est lui même cassé en plusieurs morceaux

broke into ~~many~~ several little pieces

La vue latérale de l'épave montre l'étendue des dégâts, la carlingue est cassée en plusieurs endroits

Lateral view of ~~pavement~~ wreckage shows the extent of the damage, the cabin is broken into ~~many~~ several parts

Chapter 9

Questions for Personal Reflection

Steele says, "Put on your seat belt. It may be a bumpy ride."

So on that note, never underestimate the possibility of the straight, smooth road you are currently on, to suddenly—without warning—pivot, gyrate and loop, changing your plans and your mind forever.

From a marvelous opportunity to sorrowful dysphoria, Steele experienced a personal revelation as a result of the plane crash.

Take note, for your own sake, of the lives that you have touched during your years of existence here. We all have special strengths and talents.

Mark the gifts you have used to assist people and bring them joy.

What is your fineness?

What do you recognize in yourself as a particular proficiency?

Don't wait to use those skills. Someone needs them. Someone needs to see them, hear them, touch them, smell them, taste them, experience them and enjoy them.

Share your flair, capabilities and cleverness with the world. Steele has no regrets that he did.

Begin Again, Even If You Don't Know How

Work ethic was a pronounced discipline of both Steele and his colleagues. They would continue their plans to work in Japan. Even though they experienced an unanticipated plane crash, that catastrophe did not change their plans to fulfill their assignment. Steele, his wife Lily, and Lee and Mary Stath, pulled up their boot straps and boarded yet another airplane the very next day. The Flying Marilees, were flying once again. On to Japan, to keep their word, that they would be there to see their commitment through.

"We arrived in Japan a day late. No one knew the news that our plane had crashed. Nobody knew we were coming or not. There were no cell phones. We just showed up and there we were," Steele said. "We didn't know where to go. We had to find our way to the Circus. We had to ask for directions. We would start humming Circus music to the people we would stop, and we would act like we were flying on the Trapeze so they would understand. In those days, people carried chalk and they would draw maps and that is how we found the Circus. We found the Circus and we watched the show, and Lee Stath said, 'I think we're gonna be a big fish in a little pool.' He thought we were really needed there for that little show."

Steele and his three mates worked in Tokyo, August and September of 1961, rooming in a building on the fairgrounds called Koraquein.

"It was so hot, they would put huge blocks of ice in the swimming pools. We endured and triumphed through so much, and were also rewarded and enchanted with so much on this trip. We visited three places in Tokyo–Ginza, Shibuya, and Gingaku. They have more lights than all of the lights in Vegas and Paris put together. One of the first nights we were there, we went downtown and saw this. I can't put it into words. It's just incredible. Las Vegas wouldn't make an impression at all, compared to those three places. It was just the most colorful city in the world when it came to lights," Steele said. "It was just like no-other. You had the captivating magic, but at the same time, you had to survive there. You had to eat, so when we would go to a restaurant, we would take a pencil, and draw what we wanted to eat for the waiter."

These fortunate four, walked away from a plane crash, unharmed, unlike eight on the flight who sustained injuries. Their diligent persistence got them to their mysterious destination. They beat the intolerable heat, by swimming with ice, and they drew pictures, so they could eat. Now they would be met with one more situation.

"They laughed at us. The Orientals, would clap for the clown gags, and clap for them reverently. These clowns wouldn't even be that funny, but we would do a double somersault with a full twist and they thought that was funny. They just laughed like hell.

The pirouettes cracked them up! We are risking our lives, working our tails off, and they laughed. They gave the clowns the applause. What a cultural misunderstanding! We learned, they just have a different way of thinking," he said.

...ai tử Kluger Thomas của đoàn xiệc Tây Đức (giữa) bị thương vì tai nạn rủi ro trong đêm trình diễn 1-4 đã rời bệnh viện vì gần lành bệnh. Thomas sẽ trở lại trình diễn đêm thứ sáu này.

HÌNH TRÊN : Nhân viên gánh xiệc đến bệnh viện đón Thomas về nhà. (ảnh V 10)

台灣新聞報
FORMOSA 1962

柏林高空藝術團
今日遊行明公演
在高市演畢即赴菲演出

奇技藝人

西德柏林藝術團點將錄

空中霸王飛人絕技

1962

大伯林空中서커스團

九日드디어景福宮서「데뷰」

ICE PALACE
TOKIO, JAPAN

프로그램

1、人間오토바이
2、死線을 건너는 두사람의 飛逸人
3、愉快한 自轉車旅行
4、레나드의 뮤지칼크라운
5、루디·버그의「죽음의 步行」
6、珍妙·에스키모의 점프·줄타기
7、恐怖를 모르는 주정뱅이
8、플라잉·트라페스

9、사닥다리위의 魔術
10、술렘·와이어의 챔피언
11、雄壯！大回轉「더블·트라페스」
12、즐거운「롤러·스케이팅」
13、스릴, 高空줄타기
14、爆笑와스릴,「空의 멜로디」
15、大피날레

한국일보社

曲藝中의曲藝만을公開

15種目의 프로도決定

九日부터 一般公開 觀覽券豫賣 七日부터

社告

觀覽券豫賣는 한국일보社와 朝興銀行本·支店

TAIPEI TAIWAN 1962

互相交換禮物

空中飛后瑪麗

高市稅處整風紀

嚴禁稅員 看覇王戲

Chapter 10

Questions for Personal Reflection

Steele's work ethic was off the charts.

After reading what he went through to keep his word that involved his work, how would you honestly rate your own work ethic?

Do you think a lack of genuine servitude has hurt your ability to advance in your career or with your own business?

What are some things you can do right now to increase your exertion to lead the undertakings of your career path or business?

Being true to yourself, would you be willing, like Steele was, to go to any length to work to contribute to your survival?

From Failure to Fortune

With the odds against him in many ways, Steele shouldn't have become famous, but because those odds were defeated by him, he became known by name.

"While we were performing at the Seattle World's Fair in 1962, a television studio filmed our act from the roof of a stadium. We were the Flying Marilees. They were doing an interview with Liberace too, and I heard the producer say, 'Let's do the Marilees first, and then we'll interview that piano player.' Everyone knew us. That's why they called us by name, and not Liberace. There were so many funny things that happened that way and they all cracked me up," he said. "We were always on the front of the newspapers, and the fairs would put us on the front of the programs, and just 'mention' the other performers like the singers. We always got into other shows for free, while everyone else had to pay.

I believe we are all predestined to do something. My role is to be an entertainer, because people need to be entertained. I believe in supernatural things, like what happened to Noah and what happened to Moses. I don't want to get all religious, but if I could do anything else, I would turn people on to the television show, 'Through the Bible with Les Feldick.' I've had all the fame and fortune. I don't need any more of that, and I did't need it any way. Fame is so fleeting. It's here today and gone tomorrow anyway. You ask people who the world's most famous singer is and most don't know or remember the name, 'Frank Sinatra.'

If I could use that fame as a vehicle or tool to convert people, that would be nice. A lot of athletes don't go around bragging about themselves, but they use it to help people. They use it to witness. I believe in the Bible and I believe we were created to share eternal life with God, and every time he gives us a chance, we screw up. Again, I don't want to get too religious. It's too simple and too complicated all at the same time," he said. "My idea is: I don't think I am supposed to be a virtuous person—not an alcoholic drunk like me. I think that we should witness every chance we get, about any little thing, and to point out the circumstances. Like running away from home at age 15 with a toothbrush—and surviving. The odds of that are zero. God has always been in my life. If people would stop complaining and be thankful, they would be better off. Like Charlie Chaplin said, 'He who feeds a hungry animal, feeds his own soul.'"

THE WORLDS FAIR 62
PRESENTS
THE FLYING MARILEES

June-July-August

MARY STATH: only woman in the world doing a DOUBLE
TONY STEELE: only man in the world doing a TRIPLE

Tony and Lily Steele *Lee and Mary Stath*

Chapter 11

Questions for Personal Reflection

Steele gained good fortune by his hard work, and he's always credited God for being involved in his lucky breaks.

Have you experienced good fortune by your own hard work and tenacity, or have you received good fortune by chance? Either way, how did you handle it? After reading this chapter, would you have handled it differently?

The Cycle From Poor to Popular to Poor Again

Circus life is thrilling, but in some cases, that's an understatement!

Steele said, "There was a pig act on the Gil Gray Circus. The pigs used to climb up a ladder and slide down the slide, and unroll the red carpet in the show. It was a cute act. I remember the act. The owner of the Circus owned all the acts, so he also owned the pigs. He hired trainers for the animals and the pig trainer would grab one of the pigs and the pig would grunt. They would sing Popeye the Sailor Man, and the pig would grunt.

Well, in winter quarters, at the end of the season, I got to eat in the cook house. We were all eating and everybody realized we were eating the pigs. I guess he (the show owner) didn't want to use them the next season. The pig trainer came in to eat and he said, 'Boy, this pork is delicious,' and somebody said, 'Well, enjoy it, because you are eating Shorty.' Oh my gosh, I can remember the guy's face. Oh Jeez! Real life is better than fiction."

In spite of the razzle-dazzleness and the ability to earn a living while showing off, Steele remembers more hard times.

"One year, the whole Clyde Beatty Show was parked at the fair grounds, and for some reason, things were not going well. They were in between engagements and had fallen on long, hard times. Clyde Beatty had a Liberty Horse Act of about 12 horses. He sacrificed the horses that winter, to feed the cats; the lions and tigers. Clyde Beatty loved his cats. They eat 6 days a week, so he had to," Steele said.

Steele started his successful career in the mud, but it wasn't too long, and he was performing on the red carpet. Nevertheless, he experienced his share of things not always going well.

"I remember one show, somebody from a far off asked how did the show go, and I said, 'It was very consistent. We missed every trick.' We did an especially bad act. It was when I was with the Flying Del Steele's. It was me, Betty and Billy Woods and Kim Renee. Anyway, there was a guy standing in the doorway backstage after we had a bad act, and he said, 'Here they come, the Fumbling Four.' His name was Wayne and he went out of the cannon. Any flyer knows you don't mess with them after they've had a bad show. They are not in the mood. That guy was flirting with death, let me tell you. I wanted to kill him, but it doesn't matter now. We practiced hard, got much better and worked in Reno for 10 years and Vegas for 10 years. I think that's good enough," he said.

ACROBATICS JULY 1968 (ENGLISH MAGAZINE)

THE FLYING STEELES

WE thought that readers would like to see these great sequences of Tony Steeles' superb flying trapeze act with catcher, Jaques Nicolet, and flier, Marles Tanz. Currently with Circus Scott in Sweden they are thrilling audiences with one of the finest presentations to be seen working today.

Chapter 12

Questions for Personal Reflection

Hard times, disappointments and things we don't understand can happen to anyone, anytime, anywhere, and doing what ya' gotta do, is often your only option.

Based on reading what Steele witnessed and what he personally endured, can you think back on a time when you over-reacted to what you can now determine as petty? How would you handle it now, knowing that someone else likely has it worse than you, or knowing that you indeed can improve and raise in the ranks?

Regrets from Both Sides

When the Flying Del Steeles ventured to Europe in 1963, they first went to Glasgow, Scotland, then on to Circus Krone, the biggest Circus in Europe, equipped with their own building in Munich, Germany.

Steele said, "The European show producers, they try to control everything. They say, 'You take them this year, we'll take them next year' - and so on. That's what they tried to do with us, however, I was booking the act at the time, and they had to write to me, and I didn't care what their plans were.

I received a letter from Knie, a Circus in Switzerland. We had a high level of success with the triple somersault being caught 90-95% of the time. The Knie family wrote to me and said, 'We would like to book your act for our Circus, but every patron will pay full price for a ticket and they expect to see the triple at 100%. I wrote back and said, our percentage on the triple is 93% and we're pretty proud of that. If we could do the triple 100% of the time, we wouldn't take the trouble to put up the %@#&^ net! The Knies were so mad that anyone would dare talk to them in such a manner, that we never worked Circus Knie. It is one of the best Circuses in the world, but we never made it. They thought they were a dynasty. Like they had their own empire or kingdom, that everybody should scrape down to them. They think no one should bicker, argue or even negotiate with them. They want to be in control of everything. So as you probably guessed, we never worked Circus Knie, but catching any trick 100% of the time is an impossibility. Writing back to him in the fashion that I did, was such a satisfaction in itself that it was worth blowing the whole season in Europe. We worked for every Circus, but we never worked for the great Knie Dynasty.

I did find out years later from one of the girls who worked with the Thuron Bicycle Act my wife had worked for, that the Knies regretted that loss. She married one of the Knie boys and said they were really sorry about never having the Del Steeles as part of their show."

Billy Woods, Betty Woods Reilly, Tony Steele

Acrobatics - June 1969 (English Magazine)

THE FLYING DEL STEELES

WE have followed the fortunes of Tony Steele, triple somersault flier, with considerable interest for he is an avid enthusiast for acrobatic work and a regular reader of our magazine. Those who have seen him perform are in no doubt as to his undeniable ability which ranks him as one of the finest fliers in the world.

Today after a spell with the ALIZES former partners we find him back with his former catcher BILL WOODS and here again we have a superlative performer who can by his ability get the best out of any flier.

The FLYING DEL STEELES now comprise Bill Woods catcher, Betty Woods flier, Lynn Graham flier and Tony Steele — and from all accounts their practices have indicated that this is the finest act Tony has ever been with—so it really should be great.

At present they have a long contract with CIRCUS CIRCUS in Las Vegas, U.S.A., so it will be a little time before audiences on this side of the Atlantic see them and I am sure there will be plenty of competition for their services.

The illustrations with this feature show the personnel: left to right BILL WOODS, BETTY WOODS (Bill's wife), LYNN GRAHAM and TONY and how about that costume? Under this we have a triple and double with a full twist.

Chapter 13

Questions for Personal Reflection

Have you ever burned a bridge?

Was it worth it?

If not, how can you negotiate differently, to ensure the result will turn out to be more favorable?

WHAT I WOULD DO DIFFERENTLY

"If I could go back, I would not have started smoking," Steele said. "I started about age 15, then I quit in 2000. I just thought it was a filthy habit. I was just smelling like crazy, and of course it isn't good for your health, so I quit, and when I did, I became depressed. It was like something was missing from my life. The reason I didn't quit earlier is because everyone kept telling me to quit and I hate people telling me what to do, so I kept smoking. And back then we didn't know about the dangers of cigarettes. We used to make advertisements. LaNorma Fox and Terrell Jacobs did a commercial in the form of a comic strip and they said it relaxed them and aided digestion. It does affect the person later in life. I just thought quitting was a sensible thing to do. What a waste of money; being controlled by a substance like that. I just quit cold-turkey.

Another thing I regret not doing, is when this farm boy said, 'Hey, you do three flips. Why don't you do four?' When he said that, I thought he was completel because four somersaults were completely im Nobody did anything when I was flying. Ther even any triples. Eddie Cole, he did a half-in taught myself tricks. I used to tell Billy Woods, 'Just close your eyes, make the lock, stick your hands out and I'll do the rest.' We practiced so much, we put a couch and a refrigerator on the pedestal board during practice, so we wouldn't have to get down to get anything to eat or drink. We were great, but if I knew then, what I know now, I would have tried to throw four to a catcher. But the farm boy did get me to think about the three and one half, and I was the first one to complete a three and one half to a catcher. Lee Stath caught me. Later, in 1982, Miguel Vazquez caught the first quadruple somersault," he said. "So it can be done."

Steele also said he would have kept up with paperwork a little bit better. His lack of making that a good habit, cost him a lot of money, for a long time.

"I doubled in a few Bond movies, 'Gold Finger' in 1964 and 'Diamonds are Forever' in 1971, but it wasn't until I did a movie with John Zimmerman called, 'Jonah Hex' in 2010," he said. "They offered for me to be a member of the Screen Actors Guild, and they found several thousand dollars they owed me from years back. I was just lucky. Thanks to John, I still get residuals. When I became a member of Screen Actors Guild I wanted to use the name 'Tony Steele', like I did in the Circus, because it sounds so theatrical, but they said that name was not available. It had already been taken, so I had to go with David A. Steele. I don't really like it. That is the name my mother gave me, so anytime someone says, 'David,' I say, 'Oh boy, what did I do wrong?'"

Un record du monde, mercredi, au trapèze

Tony Steele, 30 ans, 1 m. 62, 61 kilos, est acrobate depuis quinze ans.

UN corps vêtu d'un collant blanc couleur de farine se lance dans le vide. Des paillettes rouges scintillent dans la lumière des projecteurs. Un grand cri monte de la foule. C'est ce qui va se passer mercredi sous le chapiteau du Cirque d'Hiver où, à l'occasion du 10e Gala de la Piste, le trapéziste américain Tony Steele va exécuter pour la première fois au monde un TRIPLE SAUT PERILLEUX ET DEMI à 14 mètres du sol.

Tony Steele nous a expliqué en quoi consistait son numéro (notre dessin) :

1 après avoir pris son élan du haut de la plate-forme, Tony Steele effectue trois balancements au trapèze puis lâche la barre et exécute un premier saut périlleux ;

2 il tourne une deuxième fois sur lui-même en position « groupée » ;

3 à la fin du troisième saut, au lieu de s'accrocher à son partenaire par les mains, il exécute encore un demi-tour ;

4 Tony Steele est alors placé de telle manière que son porteur peut le saisir AUX JARRETS. C'est ce qui constitue la difficulté et le côté inédit de ce numéro.

(Le Xe Gala de la Piste est organisé par Louis Merlin au profit des artistes victimes d'accidents.)

Les sinistrés d'Arcueil :

« Nous sommes tous solidaires »

LES 140 sinistrés d'Arcueil qui, hier, ont été autorisés à remonter dix minutes dans leur logement pour y prendre leurs biens les plus précieux, se sont réunis dans la soirée en assemblée générale et ont publié ensuite un communiqué dans lequel ils déclarent notamment :

« La seule solution est, pour nous, le relogement immédiat et définitif pour tous. Pour l'instant, huit logements nous ont été proposés par la municipalité d'Arcueil, mais nous avons décidé ensemble de n'effectuer aucun emménagement tant que l'ensemble des sinistrés n'aura pas la garantie du relogement.

» Nous entendons agir solidairement notamment en direction des autorités préfectorales afin que les promesses de relogement soient tenues sans délai.

» Nous faisons appel à tous pour soutenir notre action. »

En deux jours, mercredi et jeudi derniers, leur immeuble s'était enfoncé de 48 cm dans la terre.

Chapter 14

Questions for Personal Reflection

As Steele looks back on things he did that affected his health, his career and his finances, does any of this look familiar to you?

We all can change things that will be beneficial to our health right now.

What is one thing you could change to improve your health today?

We can all be more daring, and not only think outside of the box, but we can be bold enough to think outside of the hemisphere that holds that box. Although Steele, as fearless as he was, didn't think there were Trapeze tricks beyond a triple. He proved that thought to be incorrect, when he surpassed it by a half rotation, and later found out that four full revolutions could be done when Miguel

Vazquez accomplished that 20 years later.

What is one thing, that you think is impossible, but wonder if it could be done anyway?

We've all had times where there was too much on our life-plates to manage, as was the case with Steele and his unknown funds owed to him for nearly 40 years.

Can you think of any investments you may have made or items of value that you may have tucked away years ago, that need to be revisited? Surprisingly, there are a large number of people who are owed monies, according to the website: "foundmoney.com." This could be your lucky day, too.

FOLLOWING THE ABNORMAL VS. FOLLOWING THE NORMAL

"Everybody thinks you have to go to college to make it in this world. If young people ask me if they should follow their dream or go to college, I would tell them, 'Absolutely, follow your dream, especially now a days.' It's important to get an education, but it cost so much money to get an education. I would say, 'Go with the Circus.' I think it's important that people do what they want to do. Why spend all that money on college, when you can never get it back," he said.

"But nothing is the way it used to be, not even the Circus. It's not as romantic and rewarding as it used to be. It's not as lavish. Those poor people who work for Cirque du Soleil–the show takes their ego away. They put a mask on them. They break them like a horse. They do take care of them though, and on that, I envy them. They don't have to drive stakes in the ground or do mud shows, but they're not troopers either. They don't have to travel in the middle of the night, set up, work, tear down, feed the animals, clean up, no–they are getting massages and an organic, vegetarian diet.

It's just different, completely different. They don't experience the hardships we did.

When we went to Europe, we decided ourselves that we were going to Europe. We put the rigging under the boat, we did our own bookings, we figured out how to pay our way over there. We did all of that on our own. We went all over Europe and the Orient, we had to figure out how to do that, and we did it.

I had partners who were afraid to go to Europe. Afraid they wouldn't have everything they needed, or understand the language; but it's the adventure; Paris, Japan, Korea. I learned that nothing is impossible. I believe nothing is impossible. I can't prove it, but I believe everything we do is a God-thing. Do what you like, you can't fail. Anything is possible.

I actually taught myself how to fly and I learned from 8 millimeter movies. I would watch myself to know what to correct and I would watch movies of other flyers. Eddie Cole was fascinating to watch. He was with the Marilees; Lee and Mary Stath. The Palacios were the big Flying Trapeze Act with Ringling Bros. at the time; in the 1950s. We went to Ringling Bros. and watched them and my jaw was on the ground. They were really magnificent."

Tony Steele doing a Double Layout with a Full Twist to catcher Billy Woods

Chapter 15

Questions for Personal Reflection

Steele followed his dream without hesitation and has absolutely no regrets for living his life that way.

Is there a dream you have which you have not put the steps in place to have it fulfilled?

Put those steps in motion today and watch what happens. Decide to make your dream come true. Commit yourself to taking action to make your dream, your life.

"You can't change your life, until you change your mind,"
Naomi Judd.

WHO ARE YOU FOOLIN'?

We've all known that looks can be deceiving. Steele experienced first-hand, that looks can really fool a person. He learned that appearances can get you embarrassment, and it can also get you the last laugh.

"He looked like a derelict, like somebody who sleeps under the bridge, but he was extremely rich—I mean really rich," Steele said, referring to Louis Stern, co-owner of Polack Bros. Circus.

"One time the performers where all standing around and bragging about their shoes, and how much they paid for this pair of pants at Tiffany's, and talking about their tiger claw jewelry, and how much they paid for things. They were just bragging up a storm about all their clothing and how much money they had. Louis Stern was there in the midst of everyone bragging. He walked up to them and said, 'See these shoes? Twenty-five cents at Goodwill. You see this shirt? I got three of 'em for twenty-five cents at Salvation Army. You see this key? It's to my safety deposit box with $20 million in it!'

I was right there. I just laughed because he looked like such a bum. They all worked for him. He knew how much money they made, because he paid them!

Here's how rich he was, I had a check from him, and I went to the bank to cash it. They said they would have to check to make sure it would clear, and I had to see the supervisor. The guy came back and said, 'Yes, we can cash this check.' I said, 'Oh really?, The check is okay? You didn't have any problems with it?' He said, 'This account says, 'Funds Unlimited.'' If you could see Louis, you would feel sorry for him," he said. "You would want to buy him a cup of coffee or something."

Tony Steele

Chapter 16

Questions for Personal Reflection

Two lessons are learned in Chapter 16. The first is based on looks: Don't trust the looks of anyone, and never underestimate anybody. That's just what Steele witnessed.

Has anyone ever underestimated you?

Did you enjoy their state of shock?

Did you notice the instant shift in power between you and the person who missed your true worth?

You may find yourself in that situation again somewhere in your life. Know that power is not a bad thing. Power is how things get done. The misuse of power is what is bad.

Make sure you remain on your toes when you feel the urge to judge someone. Judging and mis-guessing, doesn't only happen in the Circus world, it happens in your world.

The second lesson Tony saw unfold before him was the distasteful condition most people feel driven to do–brag. Bragging about one's self, one's possessions and one's talents is a destructive thing to do. We are never guaranteed those will last, and to make matters worse–there will always be someone more superior than you in any named capacity.

Be thankful for what you have, proud of your accomplishments born of your hard work and hold wise to the fact that your possessions, gifts and abilities can all vaporize in a moment, thus changing your world forever.

From Against the Odds to Against the Norm

Tony Steele—the living legacy, Guinness Book of World Record holder, first to do many high flying Trapeze tricks, the crowds' favorite, a world traveler, an over-comer, an odd-beater and so much more—has no heirs in which to leave his treasured talents; no offspring to pass down his lessons and skills.

"Nobody is going to agree with our way of thinking, but they can take it or leave it. Lily didn't want to have kids because she was from France and it had something to do with the war. She was thinking that she didn't want her children to go through what she and her parents experienced with the Nazis. She was 15 or 16 at the time the war was over.

My brother had four children so he was also doing my part in over populating the world, so I didn't want to contribute any more.

And to be more specific about that, Lily and I didn't have the maternal and paternal instincts that everyone thinks you are supposed to have. We never did want children. People would say, 'Oh, that's too bad.' No, it's not too bad. It was our choice," he said. "We did not want children. So we didn't have any. I'm being very honest. People don't understand there are some people on the planet who don't particularly want children. It's a big responsibility having children.

When Lily said she didn't want to have children, that's when we decided to get married. I told her I only have enough love for her. Some people will be appalled by that, but that's too bad, because that is the way it is."

Chapter 17

Questions for Personal Reflection

Steele lived his life, going against the norm. He met a woman who complimented him on that and agreed.

Have you ever dared to go against what the rest of society deems natural? ____________________

Following your heart is admirable, but following your gut, when certainty fills every crack—that's bold, courageous and commendable.

If you find yourself in a position of making a determination in your life, that is not what the majority is doing, take this time, right now, to decide your decision. Take that stand, and stick to it, today.

BRAVE FEAR

II Timothy 1:7—For God has not given us the spirit of fear, but of power, of love and of a sound mind.

"People ask me where my bravery comes from. They say things like, 'How did you get so brave?'

I don't look at the Flying Trapeze as a bravery thing," Steele said. "People say to me, 'Oh I saw some guys jump off a mountain with a parachute the other day. That is something you would do, Tony!'—and I say, 'No, I would never do that.'

The Trapeze is a calculated risk. A trick like the three-and-a-half, is a bigger risk. I know I can take care of myself. I see myself taking care of myself. It is not a chance. It is a risk, but it is not a chance."

Steele said sometimes, as an achiever, you do want to push the envelope and take a bigger risk, with a bigger trick, but it's all in how you think about it.

"I never think I'm gonna fall or I think I'm gonna have an accident. I think, 'What if I don't fall?'

It's just as logical for me to think that way, and to

answer people that way. I'm not going to do something where I'm gonna get hurt," he said.

Although Steele himself wouldn't do anything to get himself hurt, someone else would.

"The only time I've been afraid was when Joe Seitz got me on the high wire. We were on Circo Atyde, under their big top on their property in Mexico City called, "Calsada de Talpan." The wire walkers on the show were Gene Mendez and Joe Seitz. Gene went off to make a movie or something and didn't tell anybody, so Joe had to walk the wire by himself. Joe was the bottom man and he could do anything, so he said, 'Hey Tony, you want to go on the wire with me?' So we were on the platform and he asked me to get on his shoulders, so I did. He took a step and I said, 'Joe, what are you doing? No!, No! Put me down. Don't do it!' And he took another step and before I knew it, we were in the middle of the wire. I pleaded and panicked and then he got to the other side. I never got up there again. I wanted to kill him. That was really sick, what he did. We were at least 30 feet high; no net. I wasn't scared of the plane crash, but I was sure feared by that," he said. "I learned never to trust Joe Seitz again."

Combining all the death-defying stunts Steele accomplished, and traveling to all parts of the world with few or no incidents, Steele was very fortunate. Some daredevil performers, though, haven't been. Steele's own wife, Lily fell in Flint, Michigan in mid-winter. She had to be left behind in a hospital while the show continued to travel. She desired to have her corrective surgery in Europe. She received extensive surgery in Denmark. It was drudgery on her and Steele. According to him, the notoriety that the Flying Steeles had in those days, earned Lily a spot with the best surgical team in Copenhagen, under the direction of a Dr. Jansen.

"The point of what I'm about to say is to remind everyone that regardless of your goals, your passions, your triumphs, your successes–which you can control all of those things–there is one thing you cannot control, and that is your appointed time to leave this Earth. Performers have fallen, with and without nets. Some have died; some haven't.

Some have been young; others not. Some have had fatal accidents during performances; some during practices. Even my very, own wife Lily fell. She missed a return bar and fell into the net in a bizarre way. She damaged her leg so severely, that she was never able to return back to the flying Trapeze, even after several operations, but at least she was able to walk normally again without pain," he said. "The way I feel about it now, since I know the Bible, things are actually appointed; even our death. It says so in Ecclesiastes chapter 3. There is a time for every purpose, for every thing under the heavens. I believe, just like we have a time to live and die, everything we do has an appointment, whether we listen or not."

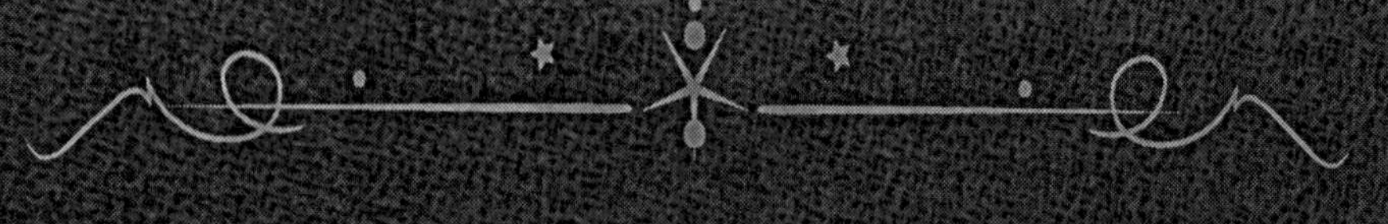

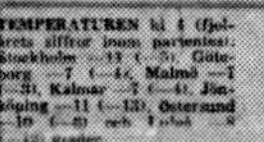

EXPRESSEN

Leva högt och farligt

Hon blev invalid i PARADNUMRET

Av INGE DAHLIN och TOMMY WIBERG (foto)

GÖTEBORG (Expressen). Cirkus är inte bara fest, färg, spänning, skratt och jubel. Det kan också vara stänk av tragik.

På cirkus Schumanns föreställningar i Göteborg sitter en vacker, [illegible] 30-årig kvinna på en av de främsta bänkarna. Bredvid henne ligger ett par kryckor.

Hon applåderar varje nummer. Det är ingenting konstigt med det. Ingen märker att hon särskilt ivrigt applåderar de tre artisterna i "The Flying Steeles", världsattraktionen som ger "samtidens mest fascinerande nummer", den tredubbla saltomortalen.

Den utförs av 27-årige Tony Steele från Boston. Han är ensam i världen om konststycket.

Kvinnan heter Lily Steele, gift med Tony. För drygt ett år sedan var hon själv med däruppe i trapetsen. Hon gjorde hisnande luftfärder som de andra 15 meter över manegen, [illegible] i strålkastarljuset och [illegible] publikens jubel med elegans.

Det kommer Lily aldrig mer att göra. Hon kan knappast gå längre. Under en föreställning i USA störtade hon och blev invalid, troligen för livet. Numera tillbringar hon [illegible] på hotellrummet.

Nervöst

När föreställningen är över väntar hon en stund tills spotlight och strålkastare slocknat. Då stapplar hon mödosamt ut genom en sidogång, stödd på kryckorna.

Expressen satt bredvid Lily på premiären. Hon var en aning nervös när Tony skulle göra sin våghalsiga luftfärd. Lorensbergs cirkus är en aning trång under takkupolen.

När det hela var över smusslade hon fram en cigarrett, tände den — trots rökförbudet — gömde diskret kryckorna under bänken och berättade:

— Det var i staden Flint i Michigan i USA. En kväll i januari [illegible]. Jag missade Bills händer — Bill är han som "fångar", hängande i benen — och störtade ner i nätet. Det räddade mitt liv, men gjorde mig också till invalid. Foten fastnade i en maska. Vid studsen vreds benet av vid knäet.

Ett sista försök

Jag låg på sjukhus i två månader i USA. Den läkare som behandlade mig i början gjorde tyvärr ett misstag. Han lade benpipan fel. Underbenet blev nästan som ett S. Titta själv. Under året som gått sen dess har jag besökt en massa läkare både i Amerika och Europa, men ingen har kunnat hjälpa mig. När vi kommer till Köpenhamn i sommar skall jag göra ett sista försök att bli bra. Jag skall gå till den bästa kirurgen som finns i Danmark.

Lily, som är parisiska, var konstcyklist när hon träffade Tony på en cirkus i Amerika. De gifte sig för sex år sedan. Hon blev fjärde medlem i "The Flying Steeles". Förutom Tony bestod gruppen av Bill och Rosalene Woods från Texas.

Ett farligt jobb

Nu är det dessa tre kvar. Trapetsartisternas yrke är farligt. Dödsstörtningar har inträffat, trots skyddsnät. För några år sedan ramlade Bill ner, slog axel och huvud i och var borta i tre månader.

— Tony jobbar för oss båda nu. När han slutat skall vi köpa en kycklingfarm någonstans. Det är nog inte så farligt att hänga i trapets. Men det svåraste av allt, det är att hantera dom här kryckorna...

Det vackra ansiktet lyser upp i ett tappert leende.

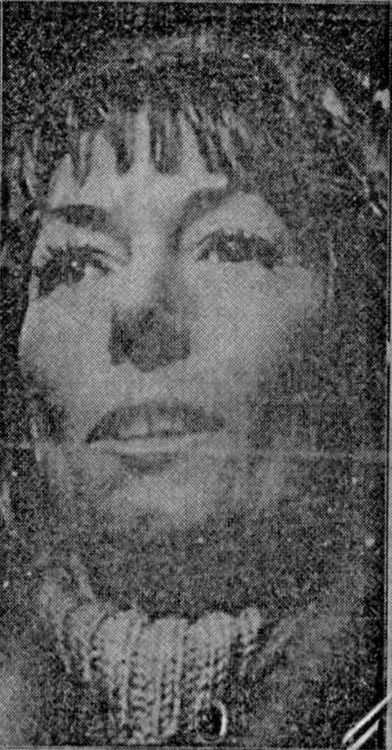

Hon darrar varje gång hennes kamrater gör den tredubbla [illegible] — hon var själv en gång en av dem. Hon störtade och nu sitter hon som invalid på parketten.

Lily Steele

Arbetet

73:e årg. Uppl. A 132 * SÖNDAGEN 17 MAJ 1964 Lösnummerpris 50 öre

VILL GÖRA DÖDSNUMRET IGEN!

Lily Steele — medlem i den världsberömda Steele-gruppen, som är den enda vilken har en rippel-saltomortal 15 meter ovan rkusmanegen på programmet — vill tillbaka.

I januari 1963 missade hon två desdigra centimetrar — föll 15 meter och blev invalid.

Drygt ett år senare fick hon besked av dr Knud Jansen på Ortopedisk Hospital i Köpenhamn: — Vi opererar. Ni skall kunna gå utan hjälp av kryckor.

Nu ligger Lily Steele med gips upp till bröstet. Hon säger:

— Jag vill tillbaka upp igen… jag kan höra cirkusmusiken.

Cirkusnumret som truppen har på programmet är världens farligaste. Tidigare har bara numrets "uppfinnare" — mexikanen Alfred Cordona — lyckats göra det. Men för hans grupp slutade det med tragedi — hans fru dödsstörtade, själv blev han invalid och tog senare livet av sig.

Bilden: Så fort det finns ett tillfälle hälsar Tony Steele på sin maka Lily.

— SIDAN 3 —

Lily and Tony Steele

Chapter 18

Questions for Personal Reflection

If you watched the video that came with this book, before you read this chapter, can you now see how Steele used his thoughts to take and conquer the risks he took?

Did you notice he trusted himself?

Steele did with the Flying Trapeze, what it takes to make it in business; trust yourself; take the risk. This scenario sounds like Bill Gates as he left college before graduating, to begin MicroSoft. Gates trusted himself too, and we have all benefited from the risk he took.

Is it time for you to trust yourself—or—to trust yourself again?

In regards to Steele's belief in designed appointments, one thing is for sure, whether we believe in appointments or not, there will be circumstances happen in our lives, that won't be in our control.

FOR THE RECORD

Although it's in small print, and tightly nestled among lots of words, Steele's name appears in the Guinness Book of World Records, which became very advantageous to him.

"It was a big risk doing the three and a half (somersault). I didn't think it was worth the risk, but I was young and foolish, and when I got into the book, that meant a lot. I did it for myself and for the record, but I never thought it would get written down anywhere.

When I went for it, I had a lot of anxiety, because you don't have a lot of time to get to the net correctly if you miss," he said. "It's extremely dangerous and I had to really think about it before I decided to take that risk, but when you are only 26 years old and very macho, you do those things. It was a dangerous thing to do, but I was thrilled to death to get into the Guinness Book, and it proved to be financially beneficial because that reputation got us a lot of work."

The degree of danger involved in the three-and-one-half somersault is so high, Steele has caught only 20 of these tricks.

"I think it's the riskiest trick there is. I would only do it for special occasions or galas," he said. "It almost got us in trouble, with mostly the people who booked us in Europe. They wanted to put that trick in our contract. I wouldn't sign it because it was just too damn scary. People are funny. If you have something, they want it. They don't care if you get killed."

Only a short month's time had passed after Steele became the first to successfully perform a 3 1/2 back-somersault caught by Lee Stath in 1962. They continued to practice this trick again while in Monterey, Mexico, working for Circo Atayde.

"You have to make split-second decisions when doing this trick. I landed on my face with my feet over my face; the worst possible way you can fall. That was my worst fear. I was terrified of it. I knew the risk and it happened," he said.

Steele was admitted to the same medical facility where injured bull fighters were often treated, putting him in good company with other gutsy individuals. He remained there for one month to receive medical care and rehabilitation.

"But this part makes me laugh because we worked 20 years for Circus Circus; 10 years in Vegas and 10 years in Reno. I did a lot of comedy flying in those two casinos, and the announcers would say, 'Tony Steele is credited for being the first to accomplish the three-and-a-half.' I was getting credit years later, for something I did in 1962. The audience would clap loudly for me and all they had seen me do, was comedy. I think they call that 'milking it.' It was 20 years before that trick was surpassed, in 1982, when Miguel Vasquez was the first man to do the quadruple. I'm not bragging, but I was the king for 20 years. It's a feather in my cap, because it took 20 years to beat it," he said.

"Anybody is thrilled and proud to get into the world records, very proud, unless you are the person who ate the most grasshoppers or something really bizarre. It made the effort worth it, and you get some acknowledgment for it. It gave our act a lot of clout.

I'm not a proud person, but when it comes to the three and a half, I believe I deserve the credit, because of the risk involved. The first time I saw my name in there, I felt very proud. I did feel that I deserved it, because that very trick is the most dangerous trick to miss and land correctly. There is death involved."

Martes 23 de Octubre de 1962 EL NORTE MONTERREY, MEXICO

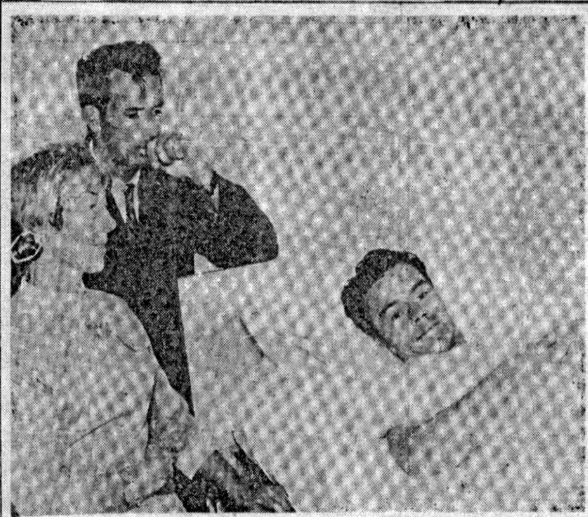

Tony Steele, el acróbata alemán del grupo "Festival Artístico de Berlín", quien anoche sufrió espectacular caída desde gran altura al practicar un triple salto mortal en el aire, rebotando en la red protectora y cayendo al ruedo de la Plaza de Toros "Monterrey". En su lecho de dolor, lo acompaña su esposa Lily Steele y su apoderado el señor Lee Stath. Tiene una lesión lumbar que le dejó paralítico momentáneamente. Es atendido por el doctor Rafael Olmos Morton, en su clínica particular.

Acróbata berlinés cae y sufre graves lesiones

Uno de los acróbatas alemanes del grupo "Festival de Berlín" que actualmente trabaja en la Plaza de Toros "Monterrey", resbaló anoche aproximadamente a las 20 horas de un elevado trapecio —del que no se precisa la altura— para caer a gran velocidad sobre la red de protección, y de la misma fue lanzado a distancia, para producirse una luxación muscular y un fuerte golpe en la columna vertebral que momentáneamente le dejó paralítico.

Tony Steele, de 25 años de edad, fue el acróbata accidentado. Una ambulancia de la Cruz Roja le recogió del sitio del accidente, trasladándole a petición del apoderado del artista, señor Lee Stath y de la esposa de Tony, Lily Steele, a la clínica particular del doctor Rafael Olmos Morton, donde fue atendido médicamente.

Según nos fue informado por elementos del grupo "Festival de Berlín". Tony cayó cuando practicaban la difícil suerte del "triple salto mortal", que nadie en el mundo la realiza en vista de su peligrosidad, cuando el acróbata, en el trapecio a una velocidad de 75 millas por hora aproximadamente, se suelta del mismo para dar en el aire tres y media vueltas y ser detenido por otro acróbata, sólo que en esta vez les falló y Tony cayó sobre la red y dada la velocidad con la que cayó, salió despedido de ella, para caer en el ruedo de la plaza.

Al ser interrogado el lesionado, por medio de un intérprete, dijo que "no podía precisar la altura de la cual cayó" ya que ésta es variable. Tony presenta golpes contusos en todo el cuerpo y una lesión lumbar que le dejó momentáneamente paralítico, pero que, según opinión del facultativo que lo atiende, podrá recuperar lentamente los movimientos de sus piernas y brazos.

En su cabecera se encuentran su esposa Lily y su apoderado el señor Stath que, no obstante que Tony no puede moverse, confían en que dada su fuerte constitución física y su juventud, pronto podrá recuperarse y volver al trapecio.

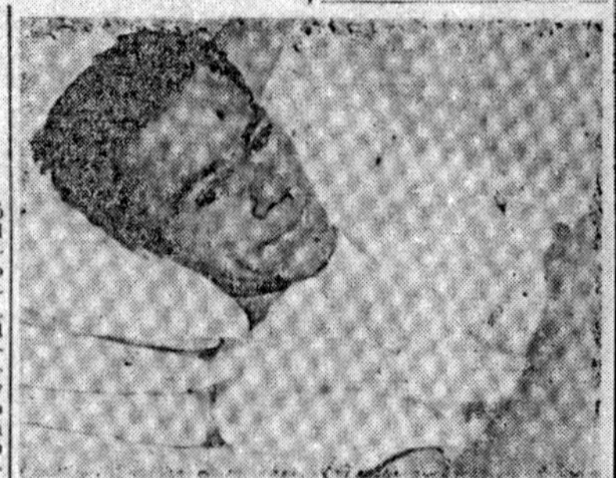

Al practicar el triple salto mortal, el trapecista Tony Steele sufrió espectacular caída desde una altura no determinada, durante la función de anoche del "Festival Artístico de Berlín". Aunque por la lesión lumbar quedó paralizado momentáneamente, confía el doctor Olmos Morton, que le atiende, que pronto recuperará los movimientos de piernas y brazos.

"Corto circuito" en camioneta, la incendia

Debido a un "corto-circuito" en el alambrado de una camioneta repartidora de refrescos, ésta se incendió parcialmente, por lo que acudieron los bomberos y pudo ser salvado el vehículo, al que sólo se le quemó el citado alambrado y los asientos.

Acudieron los bomberos en la máquina número 2, con cuatro hombres al mando del oficial Enrique Varela, concretándose las pérdidas a unos 180 pesos, sin que hubiera lesionados en el desaguisado.

Roban dos millones de pesos en México

MEXICO, D. F., Oct. 22.— La "hazaña" de los protagonistas de la película "Rififí", fue superada en esta Capital donde en la joyería "Albert" de Madero y Monte de Piedad, en plena Plaza de la Constitución, los ladrones hicieron un "boquetazo" y robaron más de dos millones de pesos en oro, brillantes, otras piedras preciosas y relojes finos.

Otros grupos de maleantes, para no quedarse atrás, también mediante "boquetazos" saquearon una refaccionaria, una relojería y una distribuidora de aparatos electrónicos, robos que en total ascienden a más de ochenta mil pesos.

GUINNESS.
BOOK OF WORLD RECORDS 1971

CIRCUS RECORDS

The following circus acrobatic feats represent the greatest performed, either for the first time or, if marked with an asterisk, uniquely. A "mechanic" is a safety harness.

Flying Trapeze	Earliest Act	Jules Leotard (France)	Circus Napoleon, Paris	12 Nov. 1859
	Double back somersault	Eddie Silbon	Paris Hippodrome	1879
	Triple back somersault (female)	Lena Jordan (Latvia) to Lew Jordan (U.S.A.)	Sydney, Australia	April 1897
	Triple back somersault (male)	Ernest Clarke to Charles Clarke	Publiones Circus, Cuba	1909
	Triple and a half back somersault	Tony Steele to Lee Strath Marilees	Durango, Mexico	30 Sept. 1962
	Quadruple back somersault (in practice)	*Ernest Clarke to Charles Clarke	Orrin Bros. Circus, Mexico City, Mexico	1915
	Triple back somersault (bar to bar, practice)	Edmund Ramat and Raoul Monbar	Various	1905–10
	Head to head stand on swinging bar (no holding)	*Ed. and Ira Millette (*née* Wolf)	Various	1910–20
Horse back	Running leaps on and off	*26 by "Poodles" Hanneford	New York	1915
	Three-high column without "mechanic"	*Willy, Baby and Rene Fredianis	Nouveau Cirque, Paris	1908
	Double back somersault mounted	(John or Charles) Frederic Clarke	Various	c. 1905
	Double back somersault from a 2-high to a trailing horse with "mechanic"	Aleksandr Sergey	Moscow Circus	1956
Fixed Bars	Pass from 1st to 3rd bar with a double back somersault	Phil Shevette, Andres Atayde	Woods Gymnasium, New York, European tours	1925–27
	Triple fly-away to ground (male)	Phil Shevette	Folies Bergère, Paris	May 1896
	Triple fly-away to ground (female)	Loretto Twins, Ora and Pauline	Los Angeles	1914
Giant Spring Board	Running forward triple back somersault	John Cornish Worland, (1855–1933) of the U.S.A.	St. Louis, Missouri	1874
Risley (Human Juggling)	Back somersault feet to feet	Richard Risley Carlisle (1814–74) and son (U.S.A.)	Theatre Royal, Edinburgh	Feb. 1844
Acrobatics	Quadruple back somersault to a chair	Sylvester Mezzetti (voltiger) to Butch Mezzetti (catcher)	New York Hippodrome	1915–17
Aerialist	One arm swings 125 (no net) 32 feet up	Vicky Unus (La Toria) (U.S.A.)	Ringling Bros., Barnum & Bailey circuit	Nov. 1962
Teeter Board	Seat to seat triple back somersault	The 5 Draytons		1896
Wire-Juggling	16 hoops (hands and feet)	Ala Naito (Japan) (female)	Madison Square Garden, N.Y.	1937
Low Wire (7 feet)	Feet to feet forward somersault	Con Colleano	Empire Theatre, Johannesburg	1923
		Ala Naito (Japan) (female)	Madison Square Garden, N.Y.	1937
Hire Wire (30–40 feet)	Four high column (with mechanic)	*The Solokhin Brothers (U.S.S.R.)	Moscow Circus	1962
	Three layer, 7 man pyramid	Great Wallendas (Germany)	U.S.A.	1961
Ground Acrobatics	Stationary double back somersault	François Gouleau (France)		1905
	Four high column	The Picchianis (Italy)		1905
	Five high pyramids	The Yacopis (Argentina) with 3 understanders, 3 second layer understanders, 1 middle-man, 1 upper middleman and a top mounter	Ringling Bros., Barnum & Bailey circuit	1941

Largest circus The world's largest permanent circus is Circus Circus, Las Vegas, Nevada, U.S.A. opened on 18 Oct. 1968 at a cost of $15,000,000 (£6,250,000). It covers an area of 129,000 square feet capped by a 90-foot-high tent-shaped flexiglass roof.

WEALTH AND POVERTY

[...]st rulers The Kingdom of Saudi Arabia derived an income of about $500,000,000 (now £208 million) from oil royalties in 1964, but the Royal Family's share was understood to be not more than £25,000,000. The Shaikh of Abu Dhabi, Zaid ibn Sultan Zaid (born 1917), has become extremely wealthy since the Murban oilfield began yielding in 1963, and by 1966 Abu Dhabi was estimated to have an income of $67,000,000 (now £27·9 million) which if divided equally would result in an income of $3,350 per head. Before World War II the income of Maj.-Gen. H. H. Maharajadhiraj Raj

G.C.M.G., C.I.E. (1895–1965), the 11th Amir of Kuwait, with an estimated £2,600,000 per week or £135 million a year. The Amir is the Head of State but since 23 Jan. 1963 there has been an elected National Assembly.

Private citizen According to a survey researched by *Fortune* magazine published in May 1968 the world's two richest private citizens were Jean Paul Getty, 77, and Howard Hughes, 64, with evaluations of $1,338,000,000 (£557·5 [illegible]) and $1,373,000,000 (£572 million) respectively. [illegible] now resident in Surrey, England, made his first [illegible] dollars, "the hardest", in his first 19 months in [illegible] business in Tulsa, Oklahoma, in June 1916, when aged 22. Getty maintains that "if you can count your millions, you are not a billionaire". More recent esti-mates suggest that the assets owned and co[illegible] Mr. Hughes exceed $2 billion (£833 mil[illegible]

Chapter 19

Questions for Personal Reflection

Are you gallant enough to fulfill your dream adventure?

Does your passion have enough value to risk your life?

Is your livelihood worth losing while you try another opportunity where the odds are unbalanced, but if victorious, would undoubtedly change the remainder of your life?

If you answered "yes" to any of those three questions, the time to make your bucket list is now. Already made one? Review it, make your vision board and visit it daily. It's time to start marking YOUR desires off that list. The "Golden Years" are the times when mental-pictures, become actual experiences.

You decide. Are you going to look at pictures all your life? – OR – Are you going to be the photographer?

Just Around The Corner

One of Steele's favorite stories happens not to be one of his own. He is fascinated by "possible positivities," and remains enthralled, with an "edge of your seat" excitement. He lives his life in this state, and says he does so because "good things happen all the time."

This treasured, true tale happened on Ringling in the late 1940s, when the show played in Madison Square Garden. The Belvedere Hotel was across the street. The Circus performers stayed there, because they knew they would be confined to the train and would be performing in tents for the rest of the season, and this would be the last chance for something really special.

According to Steele, Burt Lancaster and his partner, Nick Carvat were performers who worked on the show. They did a perch act and a bar act. Carvat was the smaller of the two, but he was the one on the bottom holding the perch; the real strongman. Cravat was only 5 ft. in height, but an incredibly rugged "powerhouse," and Lancaster needed him for the act.

"They were in the bar with the other performers one night at the Belvedere Hotel, when either a talent agent or a producer walked in and said, 'That's the man I need for my movie, "The Killers".' And that's how Burt Lancaster got into the movies," Steele said.

"They made two acrobatic action movies, because Burt Lancaster brought his partner Nick Cravat to Hollywood with him. One film was called, 'The Crimson Pirate' and the other was 'The Flame and the Arrow.' Their acrobatic abilities made great movies, but this story explains that any opportunity is just around the corner; love, a job, anything. Something can happen to you at anytime. You can be blessed beyond your wildest dreams without any warning. You just never know! Flash-bam-alacazam! It is the truth! Be ready for anything!"

Tony Steele, Circus Circus Las Vegas, NV

LAS VEGAS' ONE AND ONLY

CIRCUS CIRCUS

HOTEL · SPA · CASINO

CIRCUS CIRCUS CASINO

PANORAMA JULY 1969 LAS VEGAS

HIGH FLYING PERFORMERS AT CIRCUS CIRCUS -- The Flying Del-Steeles spin, flip and somersault through the air high above the Circus Circus casino. The trapeze artistry of (left to right) Tony Steele, Betty Woods, and Billy Woods and many other talented and dare-devil circus performers appear daily at Circus Circus. Tony Steel is the first man in the world to perform the now legendary three and one half summersault.

60s

CIRCO PRICE, MADRID SPAIN

CIRCO ROMA MADRID SPAIN

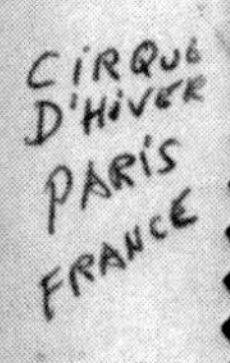

CIRQUE D'HIVER PARIS FRANCE

CIRCUS SCOTT STOCKHOLM, SWEDEN

CIRCUS SCHUMANN COPENHAGEN, DENMARK

Chapter 20

Questions for Personal Reflection

In order to have great opportunities enter your life, you have to be eager to expect them.

Are you deliberately prepared for dynamic events and tremendous good fortune to come your way?

Your willingness to believe that at any moment outrageous, incredible, colossal, eye-popping, magnificent, mountainous, phenomenal, astonishing, staggering and miraculous things can happen to change your life for the good.

Expect that your career, idea, design and dream will indeed actuate at any point. It will happen in a surprising instant. Congratulations! You deserve it. You can enjoy that smile for a long time.

Resourcefulness

During Steele's career, he took the opportunity to work with Circus Scot, aka Cirkus Scott. This show travels into the northern part of Sweden close to the Lapland area. Steele was marveled at a group of nomads called "Lappies" who roam those parts, and survive well. He gained a genuine appreciation for how they take what is provided for them, and find a way to live with it.

"They just go. They don't need a passport. They just let them go. The government just lets them roam around. They dress in very bright colors, and they live with the reindeer. That is how they exist. They use the antlers for tools and the skins to keep warm. They have found a way to live with reindeer. They don't have anything else - Just the reindeer." he said. "In Sweden in the summer time, if the sun sets at all, it only goes behind the hill for two minutes, and it comes up again. It is light, day and night. We used to go fishing at night and were able to even thread the hooks.

What I learned from this experience is that you better be satisfied with what you've got. If you find yourself in a situation where you don't have a television, a fancy car, or all the things you want, but you have reindeer, then you use reindeer. What they can do with reindeer is just incredible. They use every part of the reindeer for survival. That is all they have, and they seem to get along just fine. You have to deal with what is dealt to you, as in a card game.

From everything, I see the 'God-side.' What if there were no reindeer up there? I do see God supplying resources for all of life. Just like the bears. They know the salmon will swim up stream. The salmon is provided, but the bears still have to work for it. They have to walk down the river, walk out on the slippery rocks, balance themselves on the slippery rocks and grab the salmon in their mouths when they jump up out of the water. God provides, but we still have to go get it."

Cirkus i stan

Tony Steel — stjärnan i The Flying Steeles — gjorde dödsprånget i James Bondfilmen "Diamantfeber". På måndag kan vi se honom göra om det hoppet på Spetsamossen i Växjö — han medverkar nämligen i Cirkus Scott.

Det är cirkus i stan — Cirkus Scott är tillbaka och håller som bäst på att resa sitt tält på Spetsamossen i Växjö inför premiären på måndag. Eftersom cirkusen fyller 35 år i år har man lagt upp en jubileumsföreställning som arrangörerna lovar blir något alldeles extra.

Artister från två dussin länder medverkar i programmet, vars höjdpunkt är det nummer amerikanen Tony Steel utför: från 20 meters höjd kastar han sig ut för att landa på en minimal korkmatta. Höjden motsvarar ett ordinärt trevåningshus. Han gör också sin berömda tre och enhalvdubbla saltomortal från en trapets högt uppe under tälttaket — för den har han fått Oscarbelöning inte mindre än tre gånger. Många av cirkusbesökarna kanske redan har sett Tony Steel — på vita duken. Det var han som gjorde dödsprånget i den senaste James Bond-filmen "Diamantfeber". I övrigt finns allt man förknippar med cirkus att beskåda — vackra flickor i livsfarliga trapetsnummer, tragikomiska clowner, skickliga akrobater från världens olika hörn. Och vad vore cirkus utan djur? Fem indiska jätteelefanter, franska sjölejon, ryska vinthundar, lipizanerhästar och pudlar i lustiga och imponerande nummer — allt som hör cirkus till finns med. Och inte mindre än tjugo olika nummer upptar programmet innan det är dags för Grand Finale.

1972 SEASON

CIRCUS SCOTT
SWEDEN

Chapter 21

Questions for Personal Reflection

Could you exercise more gratefulness for the things you can claim ownership?

Are you using all of your resources to meet your goals, or to simply survive?

If you haven't done this in a while, make a list of the top 100 things you are thankful for. Surprisingly, you will likely surpass 100, and it won't take long to complete. Take this time for reflection and realization.

List the top five resources that are available to you right now, whether they are people, places or things. Make a plan, with a tight deadline to reach out to these recourses and apply them, or keep them current in your life today.

Also, pay it forward. Offer yourself to be a resource for someone, or for an organization today.

JUST WHEN YOU THOUGHT

Gutsiness was never lacking in the life of Tony Steele. With his cat-like instincts, Steele pulled off stunts, not even dared by the best of Hollywood stuntmen. He enjoyed a lengthy career that spanned a whopping 50 years of performing death-defying feats. His injuries were few and minimal; unheard of for someone in the aerial industry.

But in 2003, at the age of 67, Steele fell onto the concrete from his San Diego apparent balcony, 12 feet high.

"I was jumping from balcony to balcony to get my keys I had locked in the apartment. I had new shoes on and I missed my footing. It was silly; really silly. I broke my femur on the left leg. It was pretty smashed up. They put nine screws in my leg," Steele said.

This unexpected incident had Steele thinking he would never fly again, but after a month of walking in the pool for therapy, he tested it.

"I used to hang on the bar and ache all over. I thought I couldn't fly any more and I made my decision that I would try it. That's the only way I would find out, is if I would try it. I knew either I could or I couldn't," he said.

After the all night and day thinking about making the attempt to test his injured leg, his final decision turned out to be beneficial. Three months after the accident, Steele was able to do a double somersault to the catcher.

He said, "Don't give up hope. There's always hope. It's never over. You can be your old self again. I can't walk very far for very long, but I can fly."

Billy Tutthill, Tony Steele, Taylor Henderson
Wenatchee, WA Youth Circus

Chapter 22

Questions for Personal Reflection

Perhaps you are in a state right now where you feel you have lost the grip you had on the world's tail. How do you grab the world by the tail again? According to Steele, there is one thing you do not do, and that is give up hope.

Remember, inch by inch is a cinch regardless of what you are attempting to accomplish. By the yard, it's hard. Keep it simple and each step, attainable.

Create or re-visit one goal that will bring you closer to the skills you were once exceptional in. Can't think of one, or have put that talent in the "days gone by" category? – then reach out to someone who could use your help as a mentor. Help them feel what it's like to have the world by the tail, like you once did.

About the Author

Paula Blackwelder entered the world of live entertainment at the age of 16. With her passion for the Flying Trapeze, she was driven to soar by the encouragement of her first Trapeze coach, John Zimmerman.

She performed aerial artistry in 5 amusement parks, 2 casinos and several traveling shows for Shriners Hospitals. Her aerial work included working with troupes such as the Flying Farfans, to performing high-acts with famous sky-walker, the late Jay Cochran.

After touring the United States and performing for Circo Atayde in Mexico City, she left life on the road for entrepreneurship and family. For 10 years, she has written as a correspondent for Central Florida newspapers and wrote 5 columns weekly for 3 newspapers, formerly owned by the New York Times.

Since Blackwelder was first coached by Zimmerman 29 years ago, the couple will be wed by Tony Steele, on the Trapeze in the winter of 2014.

PaulaBlackwelder@gmail.com
www.FromGazoonieToGreatness.com

Paula Blackwelder
with Coronas Circus, Inc. For Shriners Hospitals,
Ft. Worth, TX 1990

"It must be that God loves me a little bit more than the average bear. Otherwise it would be impossible to have survived,"

Tony Steele

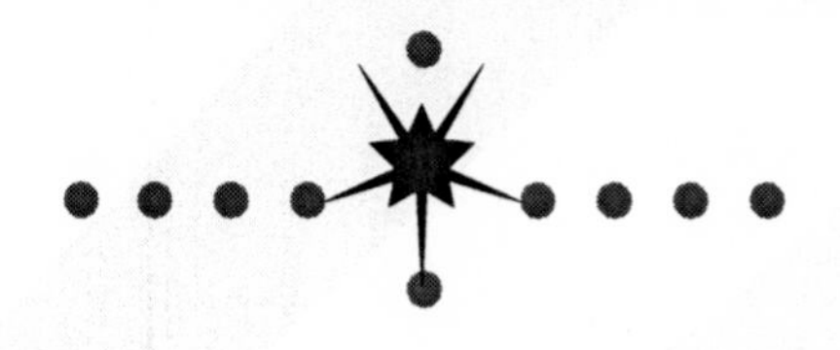

Have a dream that hasn't come true yet?
Want to make your fantasy a reality?
Need a little more encouragement to see your project through?

Lost your faith?

"From Gazoonie to Greatness" will show you how odds were beat, rags became ornate garments and determination was turned into celebration.

Go where you need to go.

Do whatever it takes.
You'll do better than just fly. You'll soar.
These are the lessons learned from a flying human, who has taught everyone else, important lessons learned from the "N" word.

CPSIA information can be obtained
at www.ICGtesting.com
Printed in the USA
FFOW05n2131031214

9 780578 151298